# THE CHURCH IN CRISIS

# THE CHURCH IN CRISIS

*Charles Moore*
*A. N. Wilson*
*Gavin Stamp*

HODDER AND STOUGHTON
LONDON SYDNEY AUCKLAND TORONTO

**British Library Cataloguing in Publication Data**

Moore, Charles
  The Church in Crisis.
  1. Church of England
  I. Title  II. Stamp, Gavin  III. Wilson, A.N.
  283'.42       BX5131.2

  ISBN 0-340-34824-0

# CONTENTS

# FOREWORD

The Church of England is constantly publicised, but little understood. There seems to be a large appetite for stories concerned with the Church, but less knowledge than has ever previously existed. Misconceptions are widespread and confusion frequently results. The official spokesmen of the Church of England often do little to correct the misconceptions. Their picture of their Church is often as misleading, though not as ill-informed, as that which the newspapers present. The authors of this book are both journalists and practising Anglicans. On the other hand, they have nothing to do with any of the Church's official bodies. They are therefore free to report what they see in their Church, and are in a position to make it comprehensible to the outside world. This book brings together their reports to give a portrait of the Established Church as it is, rather than as others fondly or ignorantly imagine it to be. The authors do not claim to be neutral in their attitudes, but they are not members of any party or faction. They write as ordinary Anglicans *for* ordinary Anglicans – for, that is to say, all the people of England who do not subscribe to another religion or to other Christian churches: these are the people who compose the Church and whom it is its duty to serve. The authors' reports depict a Church changing in a way that distances it from its ordinary members, a Church in a crisis which its leaders are reluctant to face.

*Acknowledgments*: The authors would like to acknowledge the assistance provided by His Grace the Archbishop of Canterbury; by the staff of Church House, in particular, Joy Meacham of the press office and Brenda Hough, the archivist; by the Church Commissioners; by several members of the General Synod; and by numerous clergymen and laymen.

PART ONE

# THE CENTRAL ORGANISATION

*by*

*Charles Moore*

It is generally but vaguely known that the Church of England is unique. It is an 'established' church. People have always found it hard to define exactly what this means, partly because what it means keeps changing, but everyone knows that it makes a great difference. In the first place, the existence of the Church of England rather than *a* church *in* England is the enduring reminder of England's special political independence. For reasons which were more personal than theological, not to say base and un-elevated, Henry VIII broke the English Church away from Rome. Debates about what the consequences of that break should be kept English politics busy until the settlement that followed the Glorious Revolution of 1688, but the eventual result was a harmony between Church and State and a freedom from foreign influence, which, people believed, guaranteed English liberty and was characteristic of the pragmatic genius of Englishmen.

Although it is now half-forgotten, we are the inheritors of this settlement. There is now no established church in Ireland or Wales, and the establishment in England is no longer a subject of endless political debate, but it is still true that the British constitution rests on a religious base, and that the ecclesiastical position is guaranteed by a political arrangement. If the Prince of Wales were to succeed to the throne tomorrow, he would be crowned by the Archbishop of Canterbury, Dr Robert Runcie. There would be a fuss if the work were offered to Cardinal Hume. Having succeeded, King Charles would be – as his mother is now – Supreme Governor of the Church of England. The monarch, in theory, appoints the bishops. The Queen in Parliament retains the right to govern the Church, although most of the work is handed over to the Church's own bureaucracy. The Establishment is still a fact, and an important fact, because no one has been able to propose another way of basing Church and State which would not raise far more horrifying difficulties.

But nowadays when people speak of the Church of England as a collective entity, they often mean something else again. Newspapers print things like, 'CHURCH SAYS NO TO BOMB', or, 'CHURCH BLOCKS WOMEN PRIESTS', without meaning a particular parish church or the bench of bishops. The 'Church' referred to is the General Synod of the Church of England, a body which has existed for only fifteen years. Most church-goers probably have only the haziest notion of its function and would not accept that it had authority over them. Although its more controversial debates and decisions are widely reported, it is not generally known that the General Synod governs many aspects of the Church. It may be that the Synod is the most important influence in the organisation, tone and even the theology of the modern Church, yet it is understood by scarcely anyone outside its own membership. What on earth (the Synod contains few intimations of heaven) is it?

The General Synod works from Church House in Dean's Yard, Westminster, a solid but rather dreary building designed by Sir Herbert Baker. It stands almost in the shadow of Westminster Abbey, but it has a bureaucratic rather than a religious air. The long corridors resemble offices of the Civil Service; indeed part of the building is leased to a government department. The only visible distinction between the two areas is that the government corridors are carpeted: the staff of the General Synod have to make do with linoleum. Church House also contains the circular assembly hall in which the Synod holds its London sessions. Round its ceiling is a text from the *Salisbury Antiphoner*, 'Holy is the true light and passing wonderful, lending radiance to them that endured in the heat of the conflict; from Christ they inherit a home of unfading splendour wherein they rejoice with gladness evermore.'

The Synod was inaugurated by the Queen in 1970. It replaced the Church Assembly, the first administratively self-governing body of the Church of England, which was created by the Enabling Act of 1919. The Assembly was composed of the Convocations of York and Canterbury (solely clerical bodies devoted to the discussion of doctrine, which still exist but do not matter much) and a house of laity. This arrangement was thought to take up too much clerical time and to give the laity no opportunity of discussing doctrine and worship. With 750 members, the Church Assembly was also too large. The total membership of the General Synod is 560, divided into three houses – bishops, clergy and laity. The clergy compose the lower houses of the two Convocations. The laity are elected by deanery synods which are themselves chosen by parochial church councils, for which, in turn, a small minority of church-goers vote. So 'democracy' is mitigated by a good many intermediate stages. Most 'men in the pew', let alone most nominal members or irregular attenders of the Church of England, know nothing of these arrangements. The result is that the laity which takes an interest in the Synod is untypical of congregations. It requires a special sort of mind to wish to fulfil the work of the Holy Spirit through the machinery of the General Synod.

It also requires a special sort of occupation. The Synod meets for eleven full days each year. There are three sessions, two in London and one in York. Because clergymen are busiest on Sundays, most of the sessions have to take place on weekdays. They occupy full working days. This means that almost all the lay people taking part are either rich or old, or both, and not enough of them have strong connections with unecclesiastical occupations. In the late 1940s, for instance, there were eighteen MPs in the Church Assembly. Today in the Synod, apart from those co-opted, there are only four, including John Selwyn

Gummer. There are many moans about the lack of young people in the Synod, but if one thinks of the sort of young person who might want to enter it, one should actually be thankful that he hasn't. The point is that such a body is *bound* to be middle-aged (and upwards) and middle-class, and to attract activists more than people of broad minds and independent judgment.

There is public confusion about the function and powers of the General Synod. This is because the Synod's purposes are mixed. The part of the proceedings which attracts most public attention is its discussion of general issues. A typical agenda for one day will contain one topic of general public interest, some 'legislative business' in which the Synod actually carries on the government of the Church, and less formal discussion of church matters which may later involve legislation. On Wednesday May 11th, 1983, for example, after prayers at 10 a.m., the Synod embarked on a debate of two motions concerning transnational corporations and a report on the subject produced by its own Board for Social Responsibility (BSR). It moved on to transact the 'legislative business' – the fraught question of the remarriage of divorced people in church. At 3 p.m. it debated the Actuarial Valuation of the Clergy (Widows and Dependants) Pensions Fund for the Triennium 1980–1982: Report by the Church of England Pensions Board (GS 595). Next came 'Diocesan Registrars', 'Confidentiality in Hospital Chaplaincy', annual reports, and motions from diocesan synods. Proceedings ended at 7 p.m.

Rather naively, Synod officials believe that the publicity attracted by debates on transnational corporations, South Africa, the Bomb, and so on, are important in raising the Synod in public esteem and ensuring the Church's place in the life of the nation. But they will agree that the Synod's primary purpose is to run the Church of England, and it is this central aspect of its work which needs to be considered first.

The General Synod is a law-making body. That is not a

loose description of its role in the Church: it is a legal fact. It is the only body in Britain, outside Parliament, which has the power to legislate; and it has some power to amend Parliamentary legislation. Indeed, following the creation of the diocese of Europe in 1980 and the granting to members of the diocese the right of election to the Synod, people who are neither British citizens nor resident in Britain are permitted to take part in the making of the law of England. Synod members are surprised and amused that this change was never commented on by Enoch Powell, normally the most vigilant protector of national integrity.

There are two sorts of legislation in which the Synod may indulge – a Canon and a Measure. A Canon is a piece of the Church's law which does not affect the law of England, and which, therefore – apart from a check by the Home Secretary – needs no outside scrutiny. In the discussion of the remarriage of divorced people in church, for instance, the formula which the Standing Committee tried, but failed, to introduce began with a reassertion of Canon B30, the Church's teaching which states that marriage can only be lifelong. The Synod is free to change that Canon without reference to Parliament. A Measure is a piece of Synodical legislation which does affect the law of England, and so it has to be approved by Parliament. If, say, the Synod decided that it wished to remove the right of all citizens to be buried on consecrated ground, it would have to frame a Measure. The same would be true if it wanted to get rid of the Book of Common Prayer. (Realising this, the Synod has been more cunning and has circumvented the Prayer Book by putting up various replacements for it, rather than attacking it directly.)

Because a Measure has the force of law, it has to be treated like a Parliamentary Bill. If the Synod wants a Measure, its legal adviser, Brian Hanson, has to instruct the Standing Council of the Synod, which uses the services of Parliamentary draftsmen. Drafts are taken by working parties to the Standing Committee; the Standing Committee takes them to the Synod, and so on through a series of revisions until the Measure is ready to go to the Ecclesiastical Committee, a joint committee of Lords and Commons. That Committee is not supposed to judge the merits of the Measure, but to decide whether it is 'expedient', whether, that is to say, it is reconcilable with natural justice and the constitutional rights of Englishmen. If the Committee decides that it is expedient, it then has to be approved by both Houses of Parliament. Parliament may accept or reject the Measure, but it may not amend it. The result is that almost all Measures are accepted. But there is no doubt that Parliamentary scrutiny brings a discipline which would otherwise be lacking to Church legislation.

Measures suffer from the fact that too few of those taking part fully understand the procedures and the details of legislation. Occasionally, this muddle compels Parliament to intervene. In 1983 it was forced to send back a Measure on clergy pensions because its bad drafting meant that it would have had an opposite effect to that intended. Because so many of the Church's public concerns do involve constitutional rights, and because, until 1919, all law concerning the Church had to be made by Parliament and so the connection persists, a large number of important Church enactments have to take the form of Measures. The Synod does not like this. Like all organisations, it has developed an amour-propre which leads most of its members and all of its officials to try to get more power for it. Indeed, as I shall discuss later, the Synod's resentment of Parliament has led to one of the largest, but least noticed, changes in the relation between Church and State, centring round the alterations to the liturgy.

Since the Synod is a legislative body, it needs a proper secretariat. Even its most active members cannot expect to rival the knowledge of its permanent staff because, unlike MPs, they have a forum for less than two weeks of the year. It follows that the Synod's paid servants are powerful men. And since the Synod is run on a small scale, with fewer than ten senior staff, it also follows that that power is extremely concentrated. It is generally acknowledged that one man has run the Synod almost from its foundation in 1970: he is Derek Pattinson, secretary-general to the Synod since 1972. Derek Pattinson is a former Treasury civil servant, credited with the invention of the rather unsuccessful Selective Employment Tax in the early days of the Wilson government of the 1960s. In 1968 he was seconded from the Civil Service to the Archbishops' Commission on Church and State, chaired by Dr Owen Chadwick, whose report in 1970 paved the way for the Synod's largely successful attempt to remove itself from Parliamentary control, and he joined the Synod as associate secretary-general as soon as it was set up. Derek Pattinson, who is a bachelor, is the pattern, almost the caricature, of a discreetly powerful Civil Servant. He has a large head, but very small feet which emerge from pin-stripe trousers, with the suave manner and orderly movements and appearance of one accustomed to getting his way without attracting public attention. There is no important work done in the Synod without his approval.

Derek Pattinson is secretary to the Synod when it meets. He sits next to the chairman of each session (a post shared among different bishops and other senior Synod members, many of whom do not know the procedures of the Synod or the names of the members), surveying the three-quarter circle before him and referring to a large file containing photographs of the members. He understands the composition of the unofficial 'political' factions in the Synod – Evangelicals, Anglo-Catholics, radicals – and advises the chairman whom to call. As secretary to the business sub-committee of the Standing Committee, Derek Pattinson draws up the first draft of each Synod agenda, arranging the order and influencing the choice of subjects. He is also the Synod's chief executive. He runs Church House, meeting the heads of all its departments every Tuesday morning, influencing all important appointments, and sitting on important committees. It is his job to represent the Synod in public and to other bodies. He is the Church of England representative, for example, to the British Council of Churches, 45 per cent of whose funds are subscribed by the Church of England. And, unlike bishops with their dioceses and their increasingly ambitious schemes of travel, Derek Pattinson has no flock to visit and no foreign counterparts to see. 'People expect me to be here,' he says, and he is. He stays in London and in control of Church House.

His religious and political views are naturally subjects of great interest to members of the Synod. The general opinion is that he is a moderately conservative man who probably supports the Social Democratic Party. In religion, he verges on the Anglo-Catholic, but tempered with discretion and modernism. On the ordination of women, he says that he shares the view of Cardinal Hume, believing that such a step would not be against the natural order of the Church, but that the onus is against change. In general, however, it is a mistake to look for strongly held prejudices in Derek Pattinson. He is quite clever enough to know that any hint of party bias in his decisions would reduce his power. The consistent theme which can be discerned in his attitudes is one that any student of C. Northcote Parkinson would recognise – he wants to increase the scope and authority of his organisation. This applies even in small matters. Derek Pattinson vigorously defends the appropriateness of the Synod's discussing the ethics of proportional represen-tation, on the grounds that it practises that itself and has proved the moral superiority of that form of voting. From the early days of his membership of the Chadwick Commission, he has maintained the Synodical orthodoxy that the way to preserve the Established Church is to disestablish it in all but name, making sure that all impor-tant decisions are made by the Synod, and trying to remove from Parliament, and from independent entities within the Church, all but the most vestigial powers of veto.

## THE PRAYER BOOK CONTROVERSY

The battle for this growing 'self-government' of the Church
was fought mainly over one of the most important and
controversial of all Church subjects – the modernisation of
the liturgy and the role of the Book of Common Prayer.
Perhaps 'battle' is the wrong word, for the reformers were
so skilful that very few people realised that their campaign
existed until the point when it had almost succeeded.

Throughout the twentieth century, parties within the
Church have clamoured for liturgical reform. Before the
Second World War the Book of Common Prayer was stoutly
defended by Evangelicals who saw it as a guarantee of the
Church's Protestantism. Anglo-Catholics wanted change,
and sometimes courted trouble with their bishops by inter-
polating sections of the Roman rite into their services. On
the whole, Catholic ideas gained ground in the Church,
above all the belief that the Eucharist should be the main
weekly service of the Church, and with this belief grew the
pressure for liturgical change. At the end of 1927 the
Archbishop of Canterbury presented the Revised Prayer
Book for the approval of Parliament. The Lords approved it
by 241 votes to 81. The Commons rejected it. The text was
then revised, but the Commons still rejected the Measure –
by 266 votes to 220. There was much wringing of hands, of
course, and wild talk of disestablishment, but in the end
nothing happened. The Book of Common Prayer endured,
but some bits of '1928', most notably its revision of the
rather severe marriage service of 1662, began to pass into
the use of many churches. The lesson learnt by the Church
Assembly was that future attempts at liturgical change
should not be so straightforwardly presented to
Parliament; they should be introduced piecemeal. In 1965,
Parliament approved the Prayer Book (Alternative Services) Measure. Introducing the Measure in the House of
Lords, Dr Michael Ramsey, the Archbishop of Canterbury,
used the magic word 'experiment'. Parliament was only

being asked to allow 'a limited – indeed, a very modest – degree of autonomy . . . to sanction new forms of worship . . . for limited experimental periods'. It was understood, indeed stated, that if the Church decided to adopt a new service book as a result of its experiments, it would have to come back to Parliament for approval.

This did not happen. For some years, the Church experimented. It produced Series One, which was really '1928', Series Two, a still more bowdlerised Prayer Book, and Series Three, the modern English version of the liturgy, in which God was called 'you', and people were encouraged to shake hands with one another during the service. No final form had been settled when the Synod began to work on the Worship and Doctrine Measure in the early 1970s. As was to be expected, the Synod found no fault with the Measure, giving it final approval by 346 votes to 10. What it meant was that all those matters relating to worship and doctrine would in the future be the sole property of 'the Church' (in practice, the Synod), without any Parliamentary supervision. The Measure protected the Book of Common Prayer in that it insisted that no change in the Prayer Book itself could be made without Parliamentary approval. But this concession was only granted so that the Measure could get through Parliament. The Synod realised that the Measure gave it freedom to bypass the Prayer Book without doing anything as dramatic as abolishing it.

The Worship and Doctrine Measure was introduced in Parliament by Dr Ramsey on his 70th birthday and his very last day as archbishop. The House of Lords heard him indulgently. Dr Ramsey made full use of the 'experimental' argument:

. . . the powers given under the 1965 Measure will be expiring round about the year 1980. What then? If there is no further legislation, then the only services possessing lawful authority will be those of the 1662 Prayer Book. Is it really possible or desirable to revert to that position? Is it likely that the Church

will be able or willing to present to Parliament one Prayer Book
– all at once – designed to last a long time? No . . . I think it
most unlikely.

The truth was not that the Church was mysteriously incap-
able of presenting one Prayer Book, but that the Synod,
mindful of 1928, did not want to do so.

When the Measure reached the House of Commons the
debate was more vigorous. The supporters of the Measure
tried to be as reassuring as possible. The Prayer Book, they
said, was protected: the parishioners' right to choose their
service was enshrined; doctrine was secured; and countless
new experiments were not intended. And they also
threatened (as the bishops and the Synod were threaten-
ing) that the rejection of the Measure would precipitate
disestablishment.

According to Sir (then Mr) Hugh Fraser MP, the Measure
did, in effect, produce disestablishment: 'It is asking the
House to retain the status of the Established Church while
taking away from this House the power and the responsibility for its existence.' Several other MPs pointed out that
the Measure broke down the unity in the Church which the
Book of Common Prayer assured, and placed so much
power with the Synod as to alter the nature of the Church.
'The General Synod,' said one, 'will, in fact, become in-
fallible.' According to Ivor Stanbrook, the Measure trans-
ferred control of the Church from '. . . the representatives
of the English people – to a small knot of professional and
committed churchmen . . . the Church of England is not a
piece of property to be handed over to any one group of
people'. Enoch Powell said that the Measure was a 'revolution in the constitution of the Church of England'. He
described the Church of England as the property of the
English people, existing only because it was 'by law established' – if a part of it, such as the Synod, had the power to
chop and change, the Establishment no longer made sense.
Parliament and people no longer had any guarantee of

the official character of the Church: 'It is the nature of innovation that it will not stop.'

Despite the greater eloquence of its opponents, the Measure was passed. The tactics of Synod and bishops – turning an experimental period into a condition of permanent freedom – had paid off. With the passing of the Worship and Doctrine Measure, the Synod was free, and in 1980 it was able to publish the Alternative Service Book without reference to Parliament. But the events of 1974 changed the relations between the Synod and MPs and planted the seed of complaints about the Synod which have grown more noisy ever since. MPs decided that it was important that they should know in advance what was likely to come at them from the Synod. In 1975 an informal group was set up under the chairmanship of the Bishop of Norwich. Now chaired by the Bishop of Southwark, it meets two or three times a year (the MPs would like more frequent meetings, the Synod representatives fewer) for a meagre lunch in Church House. It brings together about fifteen MPs, all with a personal interest in the Church, though not all of them Anglicans. They include Enoch Powell, Eric Heffer, Frank Field, Michael Latham and John Stokes. The Church is represented by Derek Pattinson, by Prof David Maclean, the chairman of the house of laity in the Synod, by Brian Hanson, the Synod's legal adviser and by one or two bishops. The only bridge between them is the Conservative MP, Sir William Van Straubenzee. Sir William, affectionately known as 'the Bishop', is Second Church Estates Commissioner. Appointed by the Government but not part of it, the Commissioner has to answer for the Church Commissioners in Parliament. This is his only formal Parliamentary duty, but the logic of his position (which includes an ex-officio seat in the Synod) dictates that he should introduce Synod Measures into the House of Commons. Sir William, a keen churchman and a solicitor with a reverence for order, procedure and office, is a strong supporter of the growth in Synodical power and so rather unsympathetic to complaints made by MPs about the Synod's presumption. Because of growing friction between Synod and Parliament, Sir William's regular period of questions in the Commons has become much more wide-ranging and argumentative than was originally intended. Sir William is to retire at the next election.

So each side of the meetings in Church House now regards the other with some dismay. The Synod professionals complain of the silly questions that MPs ask them, and that they are much too ignorant of the workings of the Church and too ready to intervene in matters which do not concern them. The MPs, believing that they are far more representative of the 'man in the pew', let alone of Englishmen in general, than any member of the Synod, complain that the Synod bureaucrats try to pull the wool over their eyes. Labour and Conservative MPs alike almost invariably put forward more conservative views on Church questions than those expressed by the Synod, because they believe that Parliament is the guardian of a tradition which should be handled with great care. Some amusement was caused at one meeting of the group when a Left-wing Labour MP exclaimed: 'It's bad enough having women in the House of Commons. Having women priests is something I will not stand for.' Another MP in the group says that the Synod feels 'horror and astonishment' at what the MPs say because of 'the difference between their public and our public'. Frank Field speaks of the 'feeling that, while going through the motions of seeking State advice and approval, listening to what Parliament had to say was the last thing which the Synod believed it important to do'. It was not until the introduction of the Prayer Book Protection Measure that the Synod became alarmed and felt that it should, however reluctantly, take notice.

The Prayer Book Protection Measure was introduced under the Ten Minute Rule Bill in the House of Commons by Lord Cranborne in 1981. He argued that the Worship and Doctrine Measure had failed to protect the Prayer Book as it had promised, and so the Church had not kept its side of the 1974 concordat. The Measure was voted for and a debate held. Despite an intervention in the House of Lords from the Lord Chancellor, Lord Hailsham, who said that the Measure was unconstitutional, it was given a second reading, though it was never given enough Parliamentary time to become law. In 1984, Lord Sudeley, who had acted as Lord Cranborne's counterpart in the House of Lords in 1981, tried to introduce a similar Bill as a device for setting up a Select Committee to monitor the use of the Prayer Book. The bishops attended the debate in large numbers to oppose the Bill. Lord Hailsham was again prominent, shouting angrily at Lord Sudeley for his repetition of the *Daily Telegraph*'s suggestion that the Lord Chancellor was 'bamboozling' the House, and persuading him to withdraw his Bill. These Bills, and the constant pressure from public opinion to do more to protect the Prayer Book, have had some effect, at least on the pronouncements if not on the actions of the bishops. In 1984 a number of bishops went out of their way to support the reauthorisation of revised Prayer Book (Series One) forms in speeches at the Synod, and the Archbishop of Canterbury, Dr Robert Runcie, used strong language in its praise in an article in the *Daily Telegraph* for February 23th, 1984, '. . . we dare not casually abandon our living link with the past of the Church and nation which is given us in the Prayer Book,' he said, and insisted that the Prayer Book should form a part of the life of all worshippers. He particularly emphasised the importance of its use in cathedrals and theological colleges.

But perhaps the most acrimonious and comical row between Parliament and Synod concerned a rather smaller scale matter – the Pastoral Reorganisation (Amendment) Measure 1982. This Measure was a reform of the Pastoral Measure of 1968, designed to make it easier for parishes to be closed down and amalgamated. Much of this was highly controversial, but the Synod appeared not to think that it was, and approached the Ecclesiastical Committee casually, providing unsatisfactory answers to several of the committee's questions. The Synod wanted to prevent appeals against church redundancies to the Privy Council and to remove the veto of the Advisory Board for Redundant Churches on any closure. On this second point the argument centred, the Church Commissioners keen to squash any limit to their power, the committee keen to prevent churches being knocked down.

There was impasse, until John Selwyn Gummer, a member both of the committee and of the Synod, proposed an unofficial meeting with the Synod's Legislative Committee to air views, to be followed by agreement to the Measure. John Gummer, as a matter of courtesy, informed the Second Church Estates Commissioner of the meeting. He and others were surprised and annoyed to find that at the next meeting of the Ecclesiastical Committee, several members had turned against his proposal, including the Rev the Lord Sandford. A few days later *The Times* announced that Lord Sandford had been made a Church Commissioner. At the committee meeting, a vote for acceptance or rejection of the Measure was forced and the Gummer compromise forsworn. Many members were so angry at this Synodical politicking (one of them referred to 'the most squalid little political manoeuvre I have seen this Parliament') that relations between the Synod and many MPs virtually broke down. The Archbishop of Canterbury had to step in to arrange conciliatory meetings and restore an uneasy truce.

## THE SYNOD IN OPERATION

One of the many complaints made against MPs by Synod activists is that they do not know how the Synod works, and never witness its proceedings. The fact that such an overwhelming majority of church-goers, and probably more than 90 per cent of baptised members of the Church of England, are equally or even more ignorant should perhaps give the Synod professionals pause for thought. However that may be, it *is* worth looking at the sessions of the Synod, particularly to compare them with those of the House of Commons. Here, after all, is a body which has pronounced itself competent to decide the worship and doctrine of the Church of England. How does that competence manifest itself?

It is certainly true that the standard of debate in the Synod is high. Unlike the House of Commons, the Synod chamber forms a circle, so debates are less obviously adversarial. Apart from the bishops' benches (all diocesan bishops are ex-officio members of the Synod's house of bishops), the houses of the Synod mix. Clergy and laity, each of which has 250 members, intermingle and do not sit according to membership of any party. Unlike Parliament, where time is much more plentiful, there is generally a time-limit for speeches, but each speech is listened to respectfully. And on many issues where strictly theological questions do not apply, it is common for Synod members to make up their minds and decide their votes in the light of the speeches that they have heard. On a subject like the ordination of women, where the battle lines have long been drawn and feelings run both deep and high, most debate is predetermined, but in, for example, the famous debate on nuclear weapons in February 1983, the superiority of the anti-unilateralist speeches seems to have done much to sway a Synod which it had been thought was quite likely to have gone the other way. The Government, worried about the difficulties of introducing cruise missiles into Britain, took the Synod very seriously. It put up John Selwyn Gummer to argue its case in the Synod, and Paul Johnson, one of Mrs Thatcher's most eloquent supporters in the press, wrote a long article in *The Times* on the eve of the debate which made Christian arguments for the possession and use of nuclear weapons.

As with most important sessions of the Synod, the character of the nuclear debate was emotional but polite. Where

MPs tend to stick either to details of policy or to partisan insults, Synod members like to make large speeches in the name of holy things. One speaker, for instance, talked of baptism and death as related and spoke of Hiroshima and 'the baptism of Calvary'. Another said that 'young mothers with babies and toddlers in today's world weep for their children'. And Canon Paul Oestreicher, a familiar figure at the Synod and on the international pacifist circuit, spoke of the need for 'holy foolishness' and (hinting comparison with Greenham Common) the 'women who went all the way to Golgotha with Jesus'. Emotional appeals of this sort are assured of a good reception in the Synod, but the surest path to success in Synod debates is to adopt a tone of humble moderation. Indeed there is a special adjective for it, 'eirenic' – meaning peaceful, conciliatory, vaguely holy – which is constantly used in the Synod as the highest term of praise. It was predictable that, once the Bishop of Salisbury's unilateralist motion (based on the report of his working party of the Synod's BSR *The Church and the Bomb*) had been rejected, the Synod would look for some compromise. It duly adopted the amendment moved by the Bishop of Birmingham, Dr Hugh Montefiore, and described as 'eirenic' by the Bishop of Durham (now Archbishop of York), Dr John Habgood, which forswore the first use, but not the possession, of nuclear weapons.

It is for its debates on such subjects as the Bomb that the General Synod receives most of its publicity and for which it attracts most ridicule. Every session of the Synod contains one or two such debates, often arising from reports sponsored by its BSR. The proceedings of the debates and the votes taken after them are highly predictable. Certain themes recur. All government attempts to control immigration (most notably the British Nationality Act) are condemned, as are all the works of and most connections with South Africa. Ever since Archbishop Fisher chaired the inaugural meeting of the World Council of Churches in Amsterdam in August 1948, the Church of England has been involved with the World Council's work, and Church of England money is voted to it by the General Synod. In 1978, the World Council's special fund set up under its programme to combat racism made a grant to the Zimbabwe Patriotic Front, a terrorist organisation, and refused to supervise the money to make sure that it was spent for humanitarian purposes. A huge row developed, but the Synod refrained from criticising the World Council except by 'taking note' of the controversy that the grant had caused and sending a delegation chaired by the Bishop of Rochester to visit the Council's headquarters in Geneva. The delegation's report criticised the stand-offishness of the Church of England more than the political bias of the World Council, indulging one of the Synod's favourite obsessions – that Western European churches are somehow less real than black African ones.

It is this joy at exclaiming 'mea culpa' more than any rigidly left-wing position which characterises Synodical pronouncements on social and political questions. As is perhaps not surprising from so middle-class and comfortable an assembly (surveys have shown that no skilled or unskilled manual labourer has ever been a member of the Synod), there is a disposition to see all poverty, unemployment, crime, racial hatred and urban decay as the result of the callousness of the rich. The Christian injunction to show a special reverence for the poor is elided with a quasi-socialist belief that their sufferings are produced by the 'oppressive structures of society'. Dr David Sheppard, the Bishop of Liverpool, is a leading advocate of such beliefs and has set them out in his book, *Bias to the Poor*, but they also inform all Synodical discussion. From this point of reference, the Synod's BSR sets out on its work.

The BSR is the most controversial of the various permanent boards established by the Synod. Others include the Advisory Council for the Church's Ministry (ACCM), which tries to regularise training for the priesthood (pp. 84ff), the Board of Education and the Board for Mission and Unity, the body sometimes described as the Church's Foreign Office, which tries to promote international ecumenical activities and arranges the trips of visiting cardinals, metropolitans and the like. The BSR's constituted purpose is to 'promote and co-ordinate the thought and action of the Church in matters affecting man's life in society', which naturally allows it a good deal of leeway. Since there is no clear body of thought or even of action in such a wide field, the BSR really produces its own view, rather than reflecting the state of opinion in the Church at large.

Some of the BSR's work is simply to provide a service to Synod members. If the Synod demands an urgent debate on some matter within the BSR's compass, the BSR may try to help it frame a motion. Bishops who wish to speak on a social or political subject in the House of Lords may ask for a briefing from the BSR. But for the most part, the BSR makes up its own work to spend its annual budget of £250,000. It sets up numerous working parties which call on the services of outsiders – dons, doctors, trade unionists, etc. – who are thought to be experts in the field. The working parties produce and publish reports, many of which are not endorsed by the BSR itself.

The membership of the BSR, being fairly representative, is fairly conservative. One of the problems with the public presentation of its conclusions is that people are confused about the authorship of reports. The Bishop of Salisbury's famous unilateralist document *The Church and the Bomb*, for example, was the report of a working party and was never endorsed by the BSR itself, yet, until its heavy defeat in the Synod, it was widely taken to be 'the mind of the Church' on the subject. The confusion arises because, although the working parties are commissioned *by* the BSR to report *to* the BSR, they are permitted to publish their report whether or not it is accepted.

In the summer of 1984, parties were working on 'economic values', human fertilisation and the welfare state. The list of BSR publications current in the autumn of 1983, 'Life in Society', divides subjects under the headings of 'Social and Individual Ethics', 'Industrial and Economic', 'International and Development' and 'Race Pluralism and Community'. Among the titles are *The Liverpool 8 Defence Committee, The Church of England and Racism and Beyond, British Interests in South Africa, Vasectomy, Programme for a Planet (introducing the Brandt Report), The Ethical Use of Investment Funds, Smoking, Capital Punishment,* and *Homosexual Relationships.* By no means all BSR publications adopt doctrinaire left-wing views, but there is no doubt that their arguments and conclusions are rather predictable. The BSR report on the British Nationality Act 1981 concludes: 'It is difficult to see how this legislation can be defended against the allegation that it diminishes the rights of ethnic minorities . . . and that for this reason it is implicitly racist.' The conclusion of *Facing the Facts: The United Kingdom and South Africa* (a working party report published in 1982) argues for trade sanctions against South Africa, the banning of future British investment there, and 'keeping in close touch' with external leaders of South African 'liberation movements'.

Most BSR publications accept post-war secular liberal orthodoxies about the nature of society, and make little reference to Scriptural or theological pronouncements on the subject considered. Even on those points where modern secular morality seems to be in accord with traditional Christian teaching, BSR documents more readily deal in secular than in religious concepts. In a BSR 'briefing', *The Common Agricultural Policy and World Hunger,* for instance, the author states: 'The guaranteed access to a healthy diet is a fundamental human right.' The language and concept of such rights are secular: yet the author could easily have written something like: 'Christ taught that men have a duty to make sure that their fellow men are properly fed.' Indeed the briefing does not mention Christ, the Bible or the Christian religion once.

The Rev John Gladwin, secretary to the BSR, recognises the criticisms and believes that the Board 'cannot avoid the radical Right's philosophy' any more than it could avoid Marxism when it began its work in the late 1950s. He admits that the BSR has not done enough to 'come to terms with populist Christian thinking', although his own political sympathies are with the tone of its reports.

Indeed in some of the BSR's most recent publications, such as *Perspectives on Economics* (1984) and *Growth, Justice & Work* (1985), an attempt has been made to provide a symposium of views rather than one line. But the real problem with the BSR is not the 'biased' nature of its productions, nor their rather secular tone, but the status of its pronouncements. Mr Gladwin says that the Board's work is necessary because 'social responsibility still has not grasped the heart of the Church'; yet the Board's declared purpose is to expound Church views on social matters, not to change the Church's attitudes. This confusion arises because it is not clear (except in a strictly constitutional sense) by whose authority the BSR speaks. Is it expressing the Church's view, *a* Christian point of view, or merely an informed opinion on a matter of topical interest? Is it saying something which would not otherwise have been said? Should the Church feel a duty to pay attention to what it says? These are all questions which make themselves particularly noticeable in politics because the Church's role in such areas has always been ambiguous and disputed, but similar questions should be asked of the entire work of the Synod. Indeed the questions matter more when they concern ecclesiastical matters than when they touch on politics, for they are more central to the life and nature of the Church. By what right does the Synod act?

To answer this question satisfactorily one needs to be a theologian. I am not. But by observing the operation of the Synod one can at least get some idea about how the governing of the Church is actually carried out, and whether it seems appropriate to an institution which claims to be the Body of Christ. Although it is true that on 'matters indifferent' the Synod is open-minded, and is swayed by the quality of speeches in debate, it is impossible to understand the Synod without recognising the importance of the parties within it. Although less publicly coherent, church parties are even stronger alliances than political parties because they are factions of people agreed not on vague general principles, not linked for expediency, but united on fundamental and eternal truths. They are therefore inflexible and determined. There are three groups in the Synod, although by no means all Synod members owe allegiance to any of them – the Evangelicals, the Anglo-Catholics and the radicals, the last a loose grouping united mainly by their support for the ordination of women.

Evangelicals – devotees of a missionary, Protestant view of the Church, and of the necessity of basing all Christian conduct on a strictly Biblical foundation – are growing within the Church of England. They claim the allegiance of 40 per cent of men now being ordained against a mere 8 per cent in the mid-1950s, and they are supported by approximately 120 members of the Synod (winning a somewhat larger representation in the new Synod which was elected in 1985). The Evangelical group in the Synod known, with the Evangelicals' love of nicknames, as 'Eggs', is self-consciously unstructured, but its chairman, Mark Birchall, makes great efforts to ensure that the right people come forward to speak and, still more important, are elected to the main committees and boards. (The Evangelicals claim, for example, that seven out of the sixteen members of the Synod's Standing Committee are of their party.) The group meets for supper – 'the Anglo-Catholics meet for *dinner*', one Evangelical virtuously (and untruthfully) points out – during each Synod session to decide its tactics. In practice, there are not very many issues on which the Evangelicals feel it necessary to mobilise, since few Synod reforms directly challenge their interpretation of Scripture. On the remarriage of divorced people and the ordination of women, for example, they are divided. But on those subjects on which they have organised themselves, they have succeeded. In 1965, in the Church Assembly, they opposed the introduction of prayers for the departed. In 1983 they defeated an Anglo-Catholic attempt to change the form for the reconciliation of the penitent. They have successfully blocked a move to allow the blessing of holy oils, and they also oppose all moves towards reunion with the Roman Catholic Church if this means accepting the Roman doctrine of the priesthood.

Perhaps more important than the Evangelicals' particular causes are their leading Synod members. There is the Bishop of St Albans, John Taylor, the Bishop of Chester, Michael Baughen, and, at the time of writing, the Bishop of Norwich, Maurice Wood – though younger Evangelicals are at some pains to dissociate themselves from the many pronouncements of 'Uncle Maurice'. There is Canon Colin Craston, prolocutor of the Convocation of York since 1980, and Canon Colin Buchanan, an expert on everything (to his great surprise, Canon [now Bishop] Buchanan failed to be re-elected to the Synod in 1985); and there is the Rev Michael Saward, the Vicar of Ealing, famous in the columns of *Private Eye* for his replies to articles which mock him, and a man proud of his reputation as a 'licensed gadfly'. He says that he is a suitable member of the Synod because he has the sort of mind which 'is (a) analytical and (b) a bit visionary'.

Although Evangelicals and Anglo-Catholics are supposed to represent opposite poles in the Church, and are not on terribly good terms, they often find themselves in alliance against the out-and-out reformers. As one Evangelical puts it: 'Both Anglo-Catholics and Evangelicals tend to argue about what should be as against what is', or, as one Anglo-Catholic says teasingly, they represent 'those united in revelation against those who make it up as they go along'. The Anglo-Catholics are the most tightly organised group in the Synod, partly because, unlike the Evangelicals, they find many of their tenets threatened by Synodical proposals. They form a body called the Catholic group in the General Synod. This is independent of the national Anglo-Catholic body, the Church Union, but in practice run by very much the same people. Its main organiser is Fr Peter Geldard, the general secretary of the Church Union, whose office is round the corner from the Synod in Tufton St. Fr Geldard is a young and energetic priest who has the appearance of an amiable Italian mafioso.

In the country generally the Church Union has succeeded to some extent in reviving Anglo-Catholicism. After a low point in the early 1970s, its membership has increased to nearly 12,000, 3,000 of whom (i.e. a quarter of the priesthood) are clergy. But the main work of the Catholic group in the Synod is perforce more obstructionist than positive or missionary. This is not because of a diehard mentality on the Catholics' part – though it is certainly discernible in some of them – but because many of the reforms which particularly excite many Synod members strike at the heart of Catholic belief. It was the Anglo-Catholics who managed to prevent the Synod from 'covenanting' the Church of England with various non-episcopal churches; including the Methodists. If the Measure had gone through, the Church would have been divided, possibly permanently, over the question of whether the clergy of the covenanting churches had 'valid orders' and probably over the differing views of the nature of the Eucharist.

Being the most alert of the parties, the Catholic group provides the sharpest focus to the Synod, and attracts the most attention. It has 300 Synod members on its mailing list, although it cannot claim that all of them are supporters; many bishops base their Synod diaries on the group's advance briefing. Its campaigning is thorough. When the Alternative Service Book (ASB) was being formulated, it seized the chance to insert or permit various Catholic prayers and rites which had never been permitted by the Book of Common Prayer, tabling 400 amendments. According to Fr Geldard, the group succeeded and it is possible to extract from Rite A (the modern language version of the ASB) a eucharistic structure identical to that of the Roman Catholic mass. Only three out of the fourteen theological colleges – Mirfield, Chichester and St Stephen's House, Oxford – and only a very few bishops, most notably Dr Graham Leonard, the Bishop of London, and Dr Eric Kemp, the Bishop of Chichester, who is president of the Church Union, are loyal Anglo-Catholics, but the group has influential friends in the Synod. Its members include Oswald Clark, until 1985 the chairman of the house of laity, and Canon Peter Boulton and the Ven David Silk, Archdeacon of Leicester, who are the chairmen of the houses of clergy in the provinces of York and Canterbury. Before his appointment to the see of Canterbury, Dr Runcie, then Bishop of St Albans, was a favourite with the Catholic group. Now, needless to say, his desire to hold together the different parties in the Church has lost him some of that esteem, although he remains more popular than the Archbishop of York, Dr Habgood, whom one leading Catholic scornfully dismisses as 'the liberal par excellence'.

The issue which has generated most controversy and on which the Catholic group has fought most fiercely is the ordination of women. Although Synodical rules prevent subjects being debated again and again, it is easy to circumvent them by presenting the same question in different guises. For years the supporters of women priests, centred on the Movement for the Ordination of Women, have campaigned tirelessly for their cause. Indeed the subject has been the main preoccupation of the third identifiable faction in the Synod – the radicals, organised in a less coherent body than the Anglo-Catholics, the Open Synod group. As surely as the radicals have pressed, the Anglo-Catholics have resisted. The fight follows a pattern very typical of the Synod's way of proceeding. In 1975, the Synod supported a motion which declared that there was 'no fundamental objection' to the ordination of women, passed by a simple majority, but opposed, of course, by Anglo-Catholics. Since then the supporters of female ordination have used every possible opportunity to advance their cause; and when they have been blocked on the central question, they have tried to slip in the ordination of women by less obvious means. The latest attempt to do this was in November 1983, when the draft Women Ordained Abroad Measure was introduced. This would have allowed women ordained in those parts of the Anglican Communion which admit women priests to perform their priestly duties in Church of England churches during their visits to England. Although the Measure was presented by some as no more than a matter of courtesy, it was clear that the passing of the Measure would have made it impossible to sustain opposition to women priests since women would have been celebrating communion at hundreds of altars in the Church of England. The Catholic group duly organised its opposition and petitioned the authorities that the Measure be deemed 'Article 8 business', meaning a matter which would constitute a permanent change in the service of Holy Communion, baptism, or the Ordinal. The petition was granted. Article 8 insists that such questions must be referred to diocesan synods and approved by a majority of them before being finally approved by the Synod. It also demands that the final approval has to be given by a two-thirds majority in all three houses of the Synod. The draft Measure was approved, though not overwhelmingly, but because of the Article 8 designation, had very little hope of success. The designation enraged the ordination of women lobby, always the most emotional group in the Synod, and that night's meeting of the radical Open Synod group, attended by a woman priest from New Zealand, was thick with accusations against Synod dignitaries of sharp practice. These may not have been entirely unfounded. Just as Mrs Thatcher says that she supports hanging, but would actually be much alarmed by the problems created by its restoration, so many theoretical supporters of the ordination of women in the Anglican hierarchy fear the divisions that would ensue, and the difficulties that it would raise for unity with the Roman Catholic and Orthodox churches. This means that the question is not only one of bitter dispute between Anglo-Catholics and radicals, but an extremely delicate matter for any responsible church politician. It reveals the Synod at its most contradictory – approving something in principle and then refusing to put it into practice – but also the strengths of the constitutional safeguards which mean that it is difficult to impose a really important change without very widespread consent. The latest development in the battle is the decision of the Synod of July 1985 to approve legislation to allow women to be deacons and thus, for the first time, to be members of an order of the priesthood. Proponents of the change denied that it set a precedent for women priests, but there is no doubt that it represents a move in that direction.

Because of their interest in ritual, liturgy and form, the Anglo-Catholics are masters of numerous obscure disputes and pursuers of comically arcane questions. Their most skilled soldier in this sort of territory is the Rev Brian Brindley, a frizzle-haired clergyman with an excitable manner and a church in Reading which is famous as the home of relics and ornaments flung out of less-cared-for churches. Fr Brindley is for ever popping up with questions to various Synodical officials and experts. In the Synod of November 1983, he asked:

Following the failure of 'The Blessing of the Oils' to secure a sufficient majority on 9 November, 1982, what form is available for consecrating the oil of chrism for use at the coronation of the Sovereign?

*Canon D. R. Jones*: So far as I have been able to discover, from the time of the coronation of William and Mary in 1689, the form was included in the Coronation Service itself. The prayer runs: 'to bless and sanctify thy chosen servant who is to be anointed with this oil and consecrated king'. As these words were said, the Archbishop laid his hands on the ampulla containing the oil. This prayer is part of the present coronation rite, revised by Professor E. C. Ratcliff. It is based on a prayer in the Gelasian Sacramentary.

However, in 1902, for the coronation of Edward VII, the oil was consecrated by an episcopal member of the chapter early on the morning of the coronation. This was on the advice of Canon Christopher Wordsworth, who wrote a long and learned letter to Dr Armytage Robinson. The present Queen was asked whether the oil should be consecrated during the service or before it and chose the method of 1902. The form used for this pre-coronation consecration of the oils is not known.

As to the oil itself, simple oil was used from the Reformation until 1837. For the coronation of Queen Victoria a secret formula was used by one Peter Squire. This formula has been used ever since. A new supply was made for George VI's coronation, but not in fact used, since there was enough of the old. It was kept in the Dean's study, but destroyed by bombing. For our present Queen's coronation, a new supply was prepared under the authority of the surgeon apothecary by Savory and Moore of New Bond St. Dr Don was willing to reveal that the secret formula contained oil of orange flowers, of roses, cinnamon, jasmine and sesame with benzoin, musk, civet and ambergris.

*The Rev. B. D. F. T. Brindley*: In the light of that fascinating answer which went far beyond what I had expected, can the secrets be uncovered and published, as presumably the provenance of this form of blessing makes it impossible to suppose that it does not enjoy lawful authority, and it might be of use to bishops in preparing chrism for use at confirmation?

*Canon Jones*: I have, of course, no idea . . .

An affair which reveals still more clearly the role of the Anglo-Catholics and the limitations and characteristic behaviour of the General Synod is the matter of the remarriage of divorced people in church. The subject has obsessed the Synod for many years. In 1971, it debated the Root Report on the question, and in 1978, the Synod's marriage commission, chaired by the Bishop of Lichfield,

Dr Kenneth Skelton, reported. The report was favourably received by the Synod and initiated a series of discussions in the dioceses. In July 1981, at the Synod in York, the Bishop of Winchester moved a motion in response to the diocesan synods which declared that there were times when a divorced person whose husband or wife was still living should be allowed to remarry in church (a departure from the strict existing Anglican rule), and asked the Synod to prepare 'appropriate procedures' for remarriage.

The motion was approved, but, as so often in the Synod, without any real agreement about the issues involved. Did the Synod think that the first marriage had to be rendered null before the Church could conduct a second marriage? Apparently not, but nor did it think that people had any automatic right to a second (or third, or fourth) marriage in church. It agreed that not all those who wished for a second marriage in church should be allowed it, but they were unwilling to lay down any criteria by which priest, special committee and bishop (all of whom were to be involved in the proposed procedures) would decide. Some saw the whole question as 'pastoral', by which they meant subjective and discretionary: others looked for some clear teaching by the Church. In the first debate on the Lichfield report in 1978, Oswald Clark, the veteran chairman of the house of laity, and one of the few members with a clear understanding of the Synod's limitations, warned against the Synod's trend: 'The all-pervading emphasis on relationship would seem to be proclaimed rather than argued, and proclaimed with a shrillness that at times approaches the very dangerous declaration of Jean Galot that "a person only exists as a relationship with other persons".' And he pointed out that if the Synod permitted any diversity of practice on remarriage, on grounds of the conscience of the priest, it would, paradoxically, produce more intolerance and division '. . . as is the case with episcopacy, once a diversity of practice is allowed only one viewpoint remains tenable'.

All the same, the Synod pressed ahead, and in July 1983, it approved one of the various options for remarriage procedures which the Synod's Standing Committee had proposed. This recommendation, known as Option G, left the final decision in each case to the diocesan bishop, but asked the parish priest and the couple involved to fill out various forms which would go before a committee and the bishop himself. The bishop's decision would be final and the couple would pay a fee for the service which would be non-returnable even if their petition was unsuccessful. In November 1983, the final stage of the process necessary to make 'Option G' law was passed and the Synod congratulated itself that it would have put its long-considered scheme into effect by Easter 1984. The voting was – bishops (always the most 'go-ahead' house of the Synod): 32 for to 5 against; clergy: 140 to 75; laity: 135 to 71; and 6 abstentions. According to Dr Montefiore, Bishop of Birmingham, this was one of those occasions where 'the moral intuition of the whole Church preceded the reasons for it'. The Synod was so confident of success that it rejected a motion by Mr Clark asking that Option G be referred to the diocesan synods.

At every stage of this process, many of those who voted for it were uneasy, and yet did so out of a curious feeling that the Synod should do *something*, even if there was no real agreement about the theology, or the practical problems involved. It is amusing, for instance, to follow the pronouncements of Dr Habgood. In 1978, when Bishop of Durham, he opposed any form of remarriage which distinguished between people. In 1981, he warned that 'any decision to go forward with the remarriage of divorced persons would, I believe, be deeply divisive and would lead to very different disciplines being exercised in different dioceses, and I think this would be highly undesirable.' In July 1983, he complained that the debate in 1981 had 'swept major differences under the carpet'. But in November 1983, when he was by this time Archbishop of York, Dr Habgood, after repeating his complaint that the Synod in 1981 had never agreed to the principle that marriages should be dissolved, and saying of Option G, 'I simply cannot imagine the clergy of the Church of England going through this procedure for any length of time . . .' nevertheless insisted that the Church should go ahead despite its 'foolish procedure' and 'make it work honestly'. Such a style of argument is familiar and even popular in the Synod: the archbishop's contradictory remarks moved Douglas Brown of the *Church Times* to say: 'In more than a quarter of a century of reporting governing bodies of churches I can think of no quotation more telling than that from the new Archbishop of York.' To the outside world, it sounds rather alarming that a prince of the Church counsels the Church to press ahead with something that he believes to be mistaken.

Sure enough, Option G came to grief. In between the Synods of November 1983 and February 1984 it was discussed at meetings of clergy (the people who would have had to work the scheme) of almost all the dioceses, and rejected overwhelmingly by almost all of them. Dismayed by this, the House of Bishops produced a revised proposal for the February Synod which, not surprisingly, gave rather more power to bishops than Option G had done. Like Option G, it insisted on restating the Church's teaching, contained in Canon B30, that marriage is lifelong, and yet devised a procedure for second marriage. It also refused to lay down criteria for remarriage, so the problems of 'pastoral' discretion remained. Indeed the Archdeacon of Ipswich, who carried through an amendment insisting on a *lack* of criteria, actually argued as follows: 'If the criteria were clearly known, people could truthfully say, "We fit into the criteria." Yet, in your heart, you, as the parish priest, might be thinking, "This is not the right couple to be married in church".' In other words, the 'heart' (which could easily be no more than the whim) of the parish priest should supersede any rule.

Without enthusiasm, the Synod permitted the house

of bishops' proposals to go ahead and be framed as a
regulation for the next Synod in July 1984. The proposed
regulation was attacked, however, by nine of the bishops,
led by the Bishop of Salisbury, because of its arbitrariness.
The nine proposed a proper system of nullity to allow
remarriage. Nevertheless, the proposals went through and
were referred to the dioceses for their views. But as the
dioceses discussed, more and more of them came to reject
the proposals. Thirty-two dioceses rejected them against
twelve accepting. The bishops were forced to drop their
regulation before the Synod met in February 1985. Their
solution was highly characteristic of modern Anglicanism –
bishops should be allowed to permit clergymen who
wished to do so to remarry divorcees, no clergyman being
forced to remarry a couple against his will. The *Church Times*
considered this a particularly brilliant way of proceeding:

> Thus, despite an initial appearance of disarray, the various
> lobbies within the Church have in a strange way each got what
> they wanted: the indissolubilists have prevented the Church
> from institutionalizing remarriage; those in favour of re-
> marriage may now administer (and receive) it with a clear
> conscience; and those who think that a service of blessing after
> a civil ceremony is as far as the Church may legitimately go will
> be able to opt for that too. [it added] Bowing to all these
> different pressures, though, will almost certainly lead to a wide
> variety of practice.

In the February meeting, the Synod decided to follow
the house of bishops' recommendation. It rescinded the
existing Convocation resolutions which forbade remarriage, kept the Canon which insists that marriage is for life,
and allowed individual clergy to do whatever they wanted.
Confusion and division were institutionalised. Such was
the result of fifteen years of debate.

The Synod, of course, is attacked from all sides. In
sections of the press, it is thought to be dangerously left-
wing. Among its radical members, it is considered stodgy

and unvisionary. People in parishes, so far as they think of it at all, believe that it is out of touch. Like the BBC, the Synod likes to say that because it is assaulted from the extremes it must be sitting roughly in a commonsensical middle. In fact, however, it is not the *political* position of the Synod, nor its uninspiring quality, which are its most dangerous characteristics. Only one important theme runs through the work of the Synod: centralisation. Its main work has not been to radicalise or secularise (or sanctify or strengthen) the Church of England, but to alter the way the Church runs itself so that its character is changed. The very idea of Synodical government in essential matters is hostile to the belief that the Church of England is the property of the English people (and therefore looked after them by their elected representatives). In the history of the Synod, we see a process characteristic of modern secular politics: the rise of the activist and the decline of the common man: the growth of bodies which use 'democratic' i.e. elective, procedures, yet which are remote from and even unfriendly towards the demos itself.

It is impossible to find any important area of the Church's life in which the Synod has not attempted to extend central control. Take, for instance, the structure of the parish itself, the basic and vital unit of the Church of England. The English parish system was highly independent of church bureaucracy. Parishes could not easily be abolished or merged. Incumbents (vicars and rectors) were appointed by the patron of the living who was generally either an important and ancient institution (the Crown, Cambridge colleges, etc.), or a local bigwig whose family owned the advowson (the power of patronage) hereditarily. Above all, the parson himself, once instituted, owned the 'freehold' – he had the living and the parsonage house for life, if he so wished, and could not be dislodged except, through a laborious legal procedure, for the most scandalous conduct or non-performance of his (meagre) statutory duties.

In the early 1960s, these arrangements began to be attacked. It was pointed out that half the benefices of the Church covered only 10 per cent of the population. People spoke of the clergy as members of a lump who should be moved where 'need demanded' – how defined was one of the questions unanswered. In January 1964, Leslie Paul produced a report called *The Deployment and Payment of the Clergy*, in which he recommended that the parson's freehold be abolished, that patronage should be handed over to regional ecclesiastical bodies and that parishes should be clubbed together. Pay, of course, should be nationally organised. Clergy should retire at 65. In 1967, the Morley Report, commissioned by the Church Assembly, suggested that clergymen should be retained 'on the strength' of a diocese, rather than independent in parishes. Diocesan ministry commissions would take over patronage, and the freehold would be abolished. Such views became the orthodoxy among the more go-ahead (an adjective used at that time without irony) clergy. 'Team' ministries, in which parishes were amalgamated and clergy brought into the team of a vicar in overall control, became the fashion. Even in 1983, by which time the tide was showing signs of turning, Canon John Tiller, the chief secretary of the Advisory Council for the Church's Ministry (ACCM), the Synod's body which tries to standardise the criteria for the selection and training of priests, produced a report recommending a 'strategy for ministry' which called for diocesan teams of 'specialist' clergy appointed to work with other teams from local churches.

Due to widespread opposition and the comparative slowness of Church procedures, by no means all the proposals of these and other reports have been accepted. The patronage system still exists, as does the parson's freehold. The independent parish system, though mangled, survives. But every major move by the Synod and Church Assembly has been against the existing arrangements. The Pastoral Measure of 1968 made it easier for parishes to be amalgamated and grouped according to diocesan policy, easier for existing churches to be declared redundant. The parson's freehold was curtailed by the setting of the compulsory retiring age for new incumbents. The Morley Report recommendation that the Church Commissioners become the Central Stipends Authority was accepted. Patronage was hedged about with new restrictions, and attempts, the latest partially foiled in 1983, were made to ensure that the presentation of an incumbent to a living should be made by a board of assessors pleasing to church authorities. The changes in parish structure have allowed dioceses to put in 'priests-in-charge'. These have none of the rights of the freehold and so are beholden to the Church authorities for their livelihood and are therefore less independent in their views.

Something similar has happened with the appointment of diocesan bishops. Strictly speaking, the Queen appoints the bishops. For a long time this power has been, in practice, vested in the Prime Minister. Indeed, the Prime Minister has a full-time patronage secretary to attend to clerical appointments which are in the gift of the Crown. For years this system has provoked objections among Church activists, who feel that it is an affront to the integrity and religious purity of their organisation that its most senior appointments are made by politicians. The Chadwick Report on Church and State, which also recommended Synodical control of worship and doctrine, suggested that the Church should have more to do with the appointment of bishops. In July 1974, the General Synod suggested a mechanism. In 1976, this was accepted by the Prime Minister, James Callaghan, with the agreement of the other party leaders, and the Synod duly established a Crown Appointments Commission. The Commission consists of the two archbishops, three Synod members elected by the house of clergy and three by the house of laity, and four members appointed from the diocese whose see is vacant. At the time of writing the six Synod members are

Mrs Jill Dann, Dr Margaret Hewitt, Prof David McLean, Canon Peter Boulton, Canon Colin Craston and Dr Alan Webster, Dean of St Paul's – all well-known Synod activists, most of them representative of one or other Synodical party. When a see falls vacant, the Commission meets in private for a day and a half to consider the ten or twelve names suggested. (Each member of the Commission is invited to submit names.) They begin the selection at 4.30 p.m. and have an unwritten rule to have decided by 11 a.m. the next day. They end up by narrowing down the choice to two, whom they list in order of preference. It is then for the Archbishop of Canterbury to present the two names to the Prime Minister. Although the Prime Minister is legally free to appoint someone not on the list, the convention is firm. The Prime Minister's only discretion is to select the second (and less preferred) name, although even this has happened only once. In 1981 the see of London fell vacant, and the Crown Appointments Commission recommended first Dr John Habgood, Bishop of Durham, and second Dr Graham Leonard, Bishop of Truro. Mrs Thatcher chose Dr Leonard, thereby provoking a storm of fury about 'political interference' – Dr Leonard was thought to be more conservative than Dr Habgood. In fact, if the object *was* to influence the political tone of the Church, she failed, because Dr Habgood's repudiation at London left him free two years later to become Archbishop of York. He is now the favourite to succeed Dr Runcie at Canterbury. Even in the appointment of the Archbishop of Canterbury, the Prime Minister has almost no freedom. When an archbishop is appointed, the two existing archbishops withdraw from the Commission and are replaced by one prominent lay chairman and by a bishop who is not in the running. The Commission which recommended Dr Runcie was chaired by Sir Richard O'Brien, the chairman of the Manpower Services Commission.

These changes are described by those involved in them as part of the Church's 'coming of age'; they hope that the process will be extended so that 'the Church', i.e. another commission, can appoint its own deans and canons as well. But the only clear result of the new methods is that, through the elimination of a chancy element in the system, the Church has become more likely than ever to be led by men pleasing to and probably often drawn from its politicians and bureaucrats. Not even the Commission would claim that its power has led to the appointments of saints and church statesmen who would otherwise have blushed unseen. Indeed, those appointments on whose daring they greatly pride themselves, such as Dr Montefiore to Birmingham or Dr David Jenkins to Durham, have tended to be of conventional radical theologians more admired by a small and slightly passé coterie than by church people generally.

Parliamentary irritation at some of the consequences of this growth of Church bureaucratic power boiled over in July 1984 – the same month as the consecration of Dr Jenkins as Bishop of Durham. The Synod had presented a Measure to abolish the formalities surrounding the appointment of bishops. According to an arrangement instituted by Henry VIII, the Dean and Chapter of a cathedral must elect their new bishop, but they may choose only the bishop nominated by the monarch. In the tidy and unimaginative minds of Synod politicians this procedure was so much 'farce and flummery' (*Church Times*). To many MPs, it represented an historic reminder of the separate identity of the clergy and yet of its subordination to the will of the Crown. Late at night, the House of Commons threw out the Measure, MPs taking advantage of the occasion to attack the attitudes of leading churchmen, in particular Dr Jenkins's amazing statements about the untruth of the Resurrection. Synodical bigwigs were horrified by what they considered to be a combination of ignorance and arrogance. There was heady talk of a crisis between Church and State, and of the need for disestablishment. The house of bishops recommended that the Measure be presented

again to Parliament, in order to throw down a challenge;
but when it came to the point, the Synod proved remarkably timid. In February 1985, it voted against
re-presentation of the Measure. The House of Commons
probably took note – a great deal of Synodical protest is
mere posturing. Being in the end unrepresentative, the
Synod is fundamentally much weaker than Parliament. It
realises that it must be careful how much it wields its
increased power.

In the past twenty years, then, the central administration
of the Church of England has become far more important
than ever before. And it has become far more important at
the expense of those whom activists feel that they can treat
as outsiders. Indeed, some activists congratulate themselves on the separation which has now taken place between the Church and society. According to Margaret
Duggan, the biographer of Dr Runcie, the Church became
more free in the twentieth century 'as Church and State
steadily separated and the number of church-goers who
had attended Sunday worship out of social convention
began to drop away, leaving increasingly serious and committed Christians'. This is a repetition of an orthodoxy
shared by a range of churchmen from David Sheppard,
Bishop of Liverpool, who believes that this separation
should enable the Church to criticise 'structures of oppression in society', to conservative Anglo-Catholics who
want the Church to be a strict and sacred society in defiance
of the world. The orthodoxy is also stated in the latest
history of the post-war Church, *A History of the Church of
England 1945–80*, by Canon Paul Welsby. Those excluded
from the doings of the Church are of two related sorts. One
is of leading members of secular society, above all MPs. The
other is the ordinary member of the Church of England,
sometimes a regular 'man in the pew', more often a rather
irregular user of the Church's rites. Although any such
baptised person is free to involve himself in the running of
the Church, through standing for the deanery synod, or

some still more exalted office, he is unlikely to do so because his loyalty to his particular church and parish far outweighs that which he feels towards any central form of Church government. The fact that so few people know what the General Synod is, or care to know, suggests a form of government extremely distant from most church people. And yet the Synod takes advantage of that distance to expand its scope. In matters of worship and doctrine, in the organising of parishes, the training of priests, the spending of money, the Synod has changed the Church dramatically and acted in favour of itself.

## THE CHURCH COMMISSIONERS

'By comparison with a great many of the overseas provinces of the Anglican Communion, our Country and our Church are rich, even embarrassingly rich.' So says *A Responding Church*, a document about the finances of the Church of England from 1980–3, put out by the Church Commissioners. It is true. Although few people nowadays enter the service of the Church of England 'for the money', the Church is, in terms of assets, immensely rich. The Church Commissioners, the body responsible for most of the Church's wealth, manage assets worth £1,800 million. The Church is the largest owner of agricultural land in the country and a very large owner of office property and stocks and shares. Out of these assets, the Church Commissioners, in 1983, found £114 million to pay for the running of the Church. The total cost of running the Church is thought to be about £250 million per annum, the difference between the two sums being met mainly by the contributions of church-goers.

Until the 1940s, much more financial control rested with the dioceses and the parishes themselves than with any central organisation. Two bodies, the Ecclesiastical Commissioners and Queen Anne's Bounty, were responsible for augmenting the income of the poorer benefices. In 1948, they were amalgamated by Act of Parliament into the Church Commissioners. The Commissioners' main statutory duty is to pay for the ministry of the Church – mainly, in short, the clergyman's salary, but also, increasingly, his pension.

The Church Commissioners, who work from No. 1 Millbank, a few yards from Church House and the Houses of Parliament, and just across the river from Lambeth Palace are, like most Church institutions, oddly constituted. According to the First Church Estates Commissioner, Sir Douglas Lovelock, the arrangement is 'like so many things in England – it works sensibly because people are sensible'. There is, for example, no clear chain of command. Sir Douglas is the leading salaried official of the Commissioners in that he answers to the Synod for them. On the other hand, he is not precisely the boss of the secretary to the Commissioners (also full-time and salaried), Kenneth Lamb. Formally both Sir Douglas and Mr Lamb are under the chairman of the Commissioners, the Archbishop of Canterbury, but the Commissioners themselves are like the non-executive directors of a company, only far more numerous. There are ninety-five of them – all the diocesan bishops, and many others, the great majority of whom are elected by the General Synod. (It is also provided that four Commissioners be nominated by No. 10 Downing Street and four by Lambeth Palace.) They meet only once a year at the annual general meeting, and whenever they need to appoint a new secretary. The more important bodies within the Church Commissioners are the Board of Governors, which makes the major decisions, and the Assets Committee, which contains a number of members with financial expertise. In the last resort, the Commissioners are answerable to Parliament, a function performed (p. 56) by Sir William Van Straubenzee, the Second Church Estates Commissioner.

Although they manage a huge business empire, the

Commissioners run themselves like a Civil Service department. Indeed, none of their staff has business experience. Sir Douglas Lovelock is a former chairman of the Board of Customs and Excise, and Kenneth Lamb a former director of Public Affairs at the BBC. The rest of the employees come into the Commissioners in their twenties. There is no equivalent of the Civil Service administrative grade, and so everyone has to start from the bottom and work up, gradually stepping into dead men's shoes. This makes for immobile administration, encourages some talented young staff to leave and discourages people from joining. There is no facility for drawing in people from jobs outside. Even the post of secretary is traditionally given to an inside member of the staff every other time.

As one would expect of a Civil Service department, the Commissioners follow a regular, safe and highly centralised policy. Although they are officially no more than managers of Church assets – they do not, for instance, own vicarages or churches – the Commissioners do their best to encourage uniform habits among parishes and dioceses. According to one former Commissioner, theirs is the 'typical '50s and '60s approach to fairness and equality and what would commonly be called Wetness now . . . the arguments they make are like those ICI made twenty years ago. The Church is always twenty-five years behind.'

Although the bishop is responsible in law for the payment of the clergy in his diocese, the Commissioners have gone beyond their original duty of providing the money, and now try to impose a uniform stipend throughout the country. Very little variation is now permitted. The national minimum stipend for an incumbent is set for 1985–6 at £6,900 and the maximum average for a diocese at £7,400, One or two dioceses, such as Chichester, grade their livings so that some command bigger salaries than others, but in general the uniformity is very great, with the result that bachelors are far better off than couples with families and that benefices in the north are far more difficult to fill, since most clergy prefer the south and do not suffer financially for doing so. In 1985–6, the range of salaries among the clergy was from £5,945 for an assistant curate to £13,845 for a diocesan bishop. Five senior episcopal appointments, including, of course, the Archbishops of York and Canterbury, command larger salaries – the exact sums are not revealed. On top of this, clergy get many benefits. Their heating, lighting and gardening are free of tax. Their telephone bills and secretarial expenses are paid for; their robes are set off against tax. The Church pays their rates, repairs and motoring costs and subsidises loans for them to buy cars. And their accommodation, of course, is free. The whole adds up to a comfortable, though not luxurious living for all clergymen except those with large families. Clergy are probably, for example, better off than teachers.

In recent years, however, a large number of clergy has retired, partly because of demographic trends, partly because of a Synodical/episcopal policy to discourage old clergy. (In 1975, the Ecclesiastical Office [Age Limit] Measure made retirement compulsory at 70.) And since it is much harder to persuade congregations to pay for the pensions of clergymen than to support their existing vicar, the Church Commissioners have taken up the main task of paying the pensions. The annual clergy pension in 1985–6 was £4,350 per annum, and a lump sum of £7,000 was paid on retirement to clergy who had served a full term. Of the Church Commissioners' expenditure in 1984, 22.2 per cent (£28.0 million) was taken up with pensions. One result of the growing demand for pensions has been that the Commissioners have asked that congregations pay a higher proportion of the salary of their vicar. In 1983, parish contributions to salaries, at 43 per cent of the whole, overtook the Commissioners' contributions, at 42 per cent, for the first time; and the change is very sudden. As recently as 1979, the Commissioners were paying 62 per cent to the parishes' 24 per cent. A resolution of the General Synod invited church-goers to give 5 per cent of their income to churches. This has not been achieved: the current figure is thought to be 1.5 per cent, but the recent increase in giving has still been very marked; which is all the more surprising in view of the fact that it is no longer permitted for people to give directly to their own parish church. Each parish has to fulfil its diocesan 'quota' and the diocese is responsible for redistributing the amounts.

Since the Church Commissioners believe that there should be equality between parishes and between dioceses, and since they desire to administer the Church according to a uniform national pattern, it follows that they tend to favour the selling-off of parsonage houses and the closing of churches which are too expensive to repair. Neither process can be begun by the Church Commissioners. The Church and parsonage house belong to the vicar so long as he retains his freehold – and the decision to sell a parsonage house and to apply for a church to be made redundant has to be made by dioceses. But the Church Commissioners naturally have very great influence in these matters, and do not conceal that they actively pursue certain policies.

In the case of parsonage houses, for nearly 50 per cent of whose upkeep they are responsible, the Commissioners are unequivocal. They want 'financially manageable housing stock', and they encourage dioceses to identify 'unsuitable' houses and then apply to them for permission to sell them. Indeed, it is regarded as almost immoral and socially divisive to permit the clergy to continue to live in large and old parsonage houses. The Commissioners say that about one in six of existing parsonage houses 'are not considered suitable for permanent retention'. In 1983, the Commissioners visited forty-two dioceses to encourage 'programmes for providing every incumbent and team vicar with a suitable house'. The amount which they were prepared to spend on 'basically unsuitable' houses was £16 million which represented a squeeze – the figure for 1982 was £20.4 million. Yet the cost of replacing 'unsuitable or redundant' houses is high. Old parsonage houses which are sold off are subject to a nationally uniform policy which sells them in their existing condition regardless of market circumstance. The average sum raised from the sale of such houses was £65,620 in 1984. The cost of building a new parsonage house (which is usually built according to an ugly standard model laid out in a Church Commissioners' pamphlet, *Today's Parsonage: A Place for Living and Working*) was £84,000. In 1983, 308 houses were sold, 105 existing houses were bought, and 76 constructed. In 1984, 260 houses were sold, 85 were built. Each year then, the Church parts with more housing than it buys, and pays a high price in the process. But such sales benefit the Church Commissioners because the money raised from them now goes to the diocesan pastoral account or the stipends funds whose capital the Commissioners manage. Because of centralised financing it is not possible to know whether local congregations would be prepared to pay extra to maintain a beautiful or historic parsonage house. Even if they would, such freedom would not be welcomed by the Commissioners.

In the selling-off of parsonage houses, the Church Commissioners can at least claim that they have the support of many clergy, most of whom are less adventurous than their ancestors and tend to prefer mod cons to beauty. In the closing of churches, however, the matter is not so clear-cut. It is the diocese which has to take the first step in making a church redundant. To do so, it has to put its case to the Pastoral Committee of the Church Commissioners, which prepares a draft scheme. It is for the Commissioners, after a long process, to decide what should happen to the church. It can either be 'appropriated to another suitable use', preserved by the Redundant Churches Fund (which is supported by government money), or demolished. From 1969–84, 1,002 churches have been made redundant; 548 of them have been found another use; 194 have been preserved; 260 have been demolished. In 1983, 63 schemes were approved. The Commissioners expect the current rate of redundancy to continue for the next five years.

It would not be fair to say that the Church Commissioners are always in favour of declaring churches redundant, but it is true that they have a prejudice in that direction. This they like to express in positive form. In *A Responding Church* (p. 47), they say, '. . . people, not bricks and mortar, are paramount in God's sight. A church building being declared redundant, far from being a sign of defeat, often indicates an entirely proper reuse of resources to meet twentieth-century needs.' But of course people, who are 'paramount in God's sight', often care passionately for the bricks and mortar of their church, and centre their religious lives round it; and it should also be pointed out that, despite the 'entirely proper reuse of resources', far fewer new churches are opened than old ones are closed. It is becoming more difficult to find a place to worship in the Church of England.

The principle that lies behind the policy of the Church Commissioners is that the Church is, or should be, a single administrative unit. Hence it is that a particular church or house can be described as 'redundant', and church property be referred to as 'stock', or even as 'plant'. Everything has to justify itself as part of an overall pattern. The idea that a church and its parish are an independent entity which does not need some larger justification for its existence is rejected. So it was that in 1983, the Church Commissioners produced a document known as *The Historic Resources of the Church of England*. As the word 'resources' implies, the document started from the premise that the Church's patrimony was something to be seen as a whole and to be tinkered with (or, indeed, radically reformed) as an instrument of policy. Although the document was partly presented as an exercise in 'open government', recording, for the first time ever, a sort of Domesday Book of the Church's property, it was also intended as a 'green paper' for discussion, leading eventually to action, among the church authorities.

The document started from 'the apparently inequitable

distribution of moneys available to each diocese from historic and 'other sources'. It pointed out, for instance, that the diocese of Lincoln was about fifty times richer than the diocese of Liverpool. It tried to calculate, based on assessments of personal wealth, which dioceses had the greatest 'potential for giving'; and it introduced the idea of 'liabilities' – the special costs incurred by dioceses because of the nature of their church buildings, their scattered rural populations or their urban needs. Since 1976, the Commissioners have been allocating extra funds to dioceses where they believe 'need' is greatest, and since 1981 they have allocated money year by year rather than in perpetuity, so that it is 'more readily capable of redistribution'. *The Historic Resources* even holds out a sort of inducement: '. . . those dioceses which are reducing manpower stand to receive considerable proceeds – possibly as much as £2 million in one diocese – from the sale of surplus parsonages.' Under 'Possible Ways Forward' the Commissioners suggest either 'a pragmatic approach with the minimum legislative change consistent with efficiency', which would allow for more ad hoc and voluntary redistribution by the Commissioners, or 'more fundamental action'. This second option is obscurely expressed, but it would appear to involve the pooling of diocesan assets. The pool would be administered, of course, by the Church Commissioners. The report was debated approvingly by the General Synod and submissions were invited. The next step is to be a 'white paper' urging the necessary legislative changes.

Who keeps a check on the Church Commissioners? In the last resort, as we have seen, it is Parliament. But in practice, the Commissioners more often answer, if they answer at all, to the Synod. The difficulty is that the two are too closely associated for very rigorous criticism. The Synod, for instance, is paid for not by the Church Commissioners, but by the Central Board of Finance, yet the chairman of the Central Board is Sir Douglas Lovelock, the First Church Estates Commissioner. Most of the Commissioners themselves are drawn from the ranks of the Synod, and those elected by the Synod tend to be its most vocal and thus most thoroughly Synodical characters. Although the Commissioners like to claim to be acting with the authority of the Synod (for example, the Synod passed a resolution encouraging the sale of parsonage houses), to give extra weight to their arguments, they do not regard themselves as bound by its decisions when they do not suit them. In 1982, the Synod debated a report prepared by a working party of the BSR, *Facing the Facts: The United Kingdom and South Africa*, and called on the Church Commissioners to withdraw all investment from any company with any South African connection. This call induced greater circumspection by the Commissioners, but no change of policy. The official line is now that the Commissioners' policy is 'a blend of disengagement, in the sense that they have never invested in South African companies, and constructive engagement'. The point to note is that the relation between Synod and Commissioners is cosy and, with Parliament kept firmly on the side-lines, there is no one to scrutinise and question what goes on. The Commissioners can make policy so quietly that few people discern that it is policy that they are making.

## THE ARCHBISHOP OF CANTERBURY

Whereas the Synod and, to an even greater extent, the Church Commissioners, are so anonymous that they can make many of their most important decisions virtually undetected, the Archbishop of Canterbury is extremely visible. Although he is not head of the Church of England – the monarch is its Supreme Governor – and although he has nothing approaching Papal powers, the archbishop is clearly the Church's leading figure and by far its most important public spokesman. He is the only churchman who, solely by his office, becomes extremely well known.

He is an essential presence at all the most important public occasions. He crowns the monarch and marries him and conducts his funeral. If the Church is to exert public influence, it is far more likely to do so through the archbishop than through any of its bureaucratic bodies.

The present, and 101st, archbishop, Dr Robert Runcie, divides his work into five aspects. He is, as well as archbishop, bishop of the diocese of Canterbury. In practice, he delegates the administration of the diocese to his suffragan, the Bishop of Dover, but he still has a duty to teach the faith there and make himself visible to his flock. Dr Runcie conducts the ordinations in his diocese, spending Thursday, Friday and Saturday with the candidates before their ordination on Sunday. He spends half of his weekends each year at Canterbury, where he lives in the Old Palace.

The archbishop's second task is to help with the running of the national church. He is president of the General Synod, chairman of its Standing Committee, which meets six times a year, and of its policy sub-committee. And when the Synod meets for its thrice-yearly sessions, the archbishop has to attend for at least part of the time, and to speak when he feels that a lead needs to be given on a major question. Since the Synod is constituted with so many blocking mechanisms, this means that he may well find himself speaking extremely often on the same subject. Dr Runcie, when Bishop of St Albans, was one of the early supporters of the remarriage of divorced people in church. Since then, he has felt the need to speak on the matter again and again as it struggles through its various permutations. The archbishop also chairs the Church Commissioners – though this Dr Runcie delegates to the Bishop of Rochester, only making sure to attend the meeting at which clergy pay is set for the year. Then, the archbishop has wide powers of patronage. As well as being patron of a great many livings, he is also chairman of the Crown Appointments Commission, which, in the words of one of his former staff, means that he has 'more influence on episcopal appointments than anyone since Theodore of Tarsus'. It also means that whenever a new bishop is to be appointed, the archbishop has to pass a weekend with his fellow members of the Commission deciding whom they will recommend. Since there are forty-four diocesan sees, there are generally several vacancies each year. All these chairmanships, especially that of the Appointments Commission, give the archbishop, in theory at least, more power than his predecessors, but they also take up an inordinate part of his time.

The archbishop is also, or tries to be, a 'national oracle'. This is a difficult role. Dr Coggan, Dr Runcie's predecessor, used his office to issue a 'Call to the Nation', a rather naive proclamation, read in all churches and intended to encourage people in Britain to behave rather better to one another. Dr Coggan applied to the BBC to be allowed to broadcast a short talk, in support of his Call, immediately after the nine o'clock news and was refused, which emphasised the fact that the archbishop's public role had become somewhat marginal, and perhaps encouraged Dr Runcie to say, when he succeeded Dr Coggan, that he did not wish to become a platitude machine. The public position of the archbishop is particularly delicate because, unlike the modern Royal family, he combines, in Bagehot's phrase, the 'dignified and efficient' parts of the constitution. He has to baptise Royal babies and marry princes, but he also has to say what he thinks about in vitro fertilisation or the immigration rules or nuclear weapons. In Dr Runcie's case, this problem manifested itself most acutely in the Falklands Thanksgiving service in St Paul's Cathedral, where it was thought by some churchmen that his Christian duty to condemn war made it improper for him to give thanks. In fact, Dr Runcie was rather misrepresented. He had made it clear that he thought Britain justified in fighting the Falklands war, and his sermon only spoke of all war as a symptom of 'failure' rather than arguing for pacifism; but the authorities of the Cathedral did their best to keep the service critical of British policy and so caused widespread offence and unfair attacks on the archbishop.

The natural forum for the Archbishop of Canterbury to put forward a view on national questions is the House of Lords, in which he sits, with other bishops, ex officio. Dr Runcie does not use the Lords frequently, going there only when he intends to speak, rather than sitting on the benches to listen; but through his lay assistant at Lambeth Palace he organises an informal whips' office. Bishops are assigned portfolios about which they are thought to be knowledgeable and are strongly encouraged to attend the relevant debates. Dr Runcie himself speaks on major moral issues, on questions where he believes the 'world family' of Christians can challenge insular attitudes, and on occasions when he believes that the abusive language of public debate needs to be calmed down. Because of his role as a non-party commentator on political events, the archbishop finds it easy to bring together important representatives of different sides of arguments. He often holds supper parties at Lambeth Palace to do this, before making a public pronouncement on some matter of the hour. He also has some contact with MPs over questions concerning Church government, and ready access to the Prime Minister.

The archbishop's fourth function is his headship of the Anglican Communion. This curious body grew out of the retreat of the Church of England abroad, rather as the Commonwealth grew out of the end of British imperial rule. The Archbishop of Canterbury is head of the Anglican Communion just as the Queen is head of the Commonwealth, and, like the Queen, takes the concept rather more seriously than most citizens of the countries involved. Every three years, he has to attend a meeting of the Anglican Consultative Council (the latest, in 1984, was in Nigeria), and each year he spends several weeks travelling to far-flung parts of the Communion such as New Zealand,

Nigeria and the West Indies. The Anglican Communion causes some embarrassments since it has no discipline comparable to that of the Roman Church, with the result that there is a wide divergence of practice within it. Controversy rages at present, for example, about relations between those parts of the Communion which have ordained women and those which have not. But one compensation of the archbishop's travels is that whichever country he visits, he is extremely welcome. Tens of thousands of Nigerians wait for hours to greet him, whereas in Britain he could pass almost unnoticed wherever he goes. Dr Runcie spends about six weeks of the year on Anglican Communion travel, sometimes combining it with his fifth function, the ecumenical gathering. One unfortunate side-effect of the better relations between churches has been that those churches' dignitaries have to spend a great deal of time meeting one another. They attend each other's services and arrange reciprocal visits. In 1983 Dr Runcie felt it necessary to spend more than two weeks at the World Council of Churches Assembly in Vancouver. All this is time-consuming. What with the 'ecumenical dimension' and the Anglican Communion, Dr Runcie probably spends almost a quarter of his time on work not directly concerned with the Church of England.

The great majority of this work is fairly new. Until thirty years ago, no Archbishop of Canterbury travelled very much. (Dr Lang, for instance, confined his trips to Mediterranean cruises on the yacht of the American millionaire, J. Pierpont Morgan.) Ecumenism had hardly been born. The enthusiasm for conferences and committees, though growing, had not yet become a mania. When this is added to the archbishop's increased formal role in the government of the Church of England, it means that a modern archbishop is roughly twice as busy as his pre-war predecessors. It follows that a modern archbishop is likely to be more remarkable for his incessant activity than for the profundity of his thought or the holiness of his life.

Despite the extra burdens, it remains true that the Archbishop of Canterbury, in the words of William Temple, the most famous of twentieth-century archbishops, does 'the work of a prime minister with the staff of a headmaster'. Although this means that any archbishop finds himself overstretched, it has the great advantage over Millbank and Church House across the river that moves can be made swiftly and under personal direction. There is very little continuity between succeeding archbishops. Indeed the appointing authorities, obsessed by the need for balance in the Church, generally go for discontinuity. Dr Ramsey was other-worldly where Dr Fisher was practical. Dr Coggan was conservative where Dr Ramsey was radical, Dr Runcie is High Church where Dr Coggan was Low Church. An incoming archbishop inherits no senior staff: when the Runcies moved into Lambeth Palace, for example, they got little more than some friendly advice about curtains from Mrs Coggan. Each archbishop, in short, has to make it up as he goes along.

He lives and works in Lambeth Palace which, apart from its mediaeval gatehouse, is a surprisingly unattractive Victorian building. Its large garden has a rather unloved and institutional air, and many of the rooms, which are sparsely furnished, act as ill-adapted offices. The Runcies live on the second floor, their only domestic help a cook and a cleaning woman. The Archbishop's senior staff – all personally appointed – is very small. Its chief, through whom others arrange to see the archbishop, is Ronald Gordon, formerly Bishop of Portsmouth. Dr Runcie also has a lay assistant, a research assistant, and Terry Waite, the gigantic, bearded assistant for Anglican Communion affairs, who is famous for his rescue of missionaries imprisoned by the Ayatollah Khomeini and of the Britons in Libya in 1985. The Archbishop has a personal chaplain, and an assistant chaplain at Canterbury, an appointments secretary (who travels the country scouting for suitable future bishops), an ecumenical officer and a press officer.

Dr Runcie is extremely well suited to the current ideal of an active archbishop. He is certainly the best manager in the job since Dr Fisher. Throughout his career, as principal of Cuddesdon Theological College, as Bishop of St Albans, and now at Canterbury, Dr Runcie has won a reputation for competence, balance and an amazing capacity for work. In one two-week visit to Nigeria, for example, he visited thirteen cities and delivered sixty-four speeches. Dr Runcie is not, like Dr Ramsey, a scholar, nor, like Dr Coggan, essentially a parish priest. He is an extremely well-organised man with a strong competitive and conscientious urge which drives him to enormous effort. According to his staff, his most characteristic phrase is 'on to the next thing', seldom pausing for celebration or relaxation.

How has Dr Runcie chosen to use his position? He was appointed in 1980 when he was almost 59, and so he had eleven years – longer than Dr Coggan – to make his mark. He is still only half-way through his primacy. It seems that he has decided to use his time to consolidate. Among twentieth-century archbishops, Dr Runcie is most often compared to Randall Davidson, who was said to sit on the fence with both ears to the ground and who did so, with great skill, for more than twenty years. Dr Runcie has neither the originality nor the arrogance to plunge the Church of England into a period of precipitate change such as it underwent in the 1960s and 1970s. He is very keen, for example, that liturgical experiment should now cease. He has launched a number of eloquent defences of the Book of Common Prayer (he always uses the Prayer Book for Morning Prayer at seven thirty in his private chapel at Lambeth), and he is also worried by the division of practice and doctrine produced by so much liturgical variety in a Church which has always been based on a common prayer book rather than a common confession. He is also opposed to moves to separate Church and State still further, which would give more power to Church bureaucrats. He is rather irritated by the extent and tone of Synodical government,

noticing that sister churches in the Anglican Communion
manage perfectly well with far fewer sessions: he does not
express public disapproval, but instead cuts his attendance
at Synodical committees and sessions. In politics and theology, Dr Runcie is a liberal conservative, more moved by
the need for continuity than by that for sudden change; but
he thinks it more important to keep level with opinion in
the Church than to challenge it. So, for instance, although
he is inclined to oppose the ordination of women to the
priesthood, he is preparing to accept it gracefully because
he thinks – on what evidence is not very clear – that it is
wanted by the Church and will inevitably come.

Dr Runcie's approach was most severely tested by two
events which coincided in 1984 – the year-long miners'
strike, which ended in March 1985, and the appointment of
Dr David Jenkins as Bishop of Durham. Both these events
provoked fierce passions, and both, after a time, inter-
twined when Dr Jenkins started to deliver his views on
political subjects and what should be done to solve the coal
dispute. From the moment of his appointment, Dr Jenkins
rushed into theological controversy, casting doubt on the
Virgin Birth and on the Resurrection itself. He seemed quite
unabashed by the criticisms which his rather offhand and
off-the-cuff remarks provoked, and was consecrated
Bishop of Durham, despite petitions against him and some
interruptions of the service, in July 1984. Three days later,
York Minster – where the consecration had taken place –
was badly damaged by fire. There were many who were not
slow to suggest that this disaster might reflect God's views
about Dr Jenkins's consecration (although it was not
pointed out that these were also the last days in office of Dr
Jasper, the Dean of York and chief author of the Alternative
Service Book, and so the Almighty might have been trying
to get 'two for the price of one'). Dr Runcie, of course,
visited the Minster and encouraged the rescue work.
According to his biographer, Margaret Duggan, reporting
his visit in the *Church Times*, he 'firmly refuted [it would

have been less presumptuous to have said "denied"] a suggestion that the fire might have been caused by divine anger at the consecration of Dr Jenkins'. This was the archbishop's baptism of fire. Since then, he has become used to handling questions about Dr Jenkins.

Only a fortnight or so after his escape from the lightning, Dr Jenkins spoke out once more, suggesting that the disciples might have 'pinched' the body of Christ from the Tomb. In his Easter sermon the following year, he elaborated on this theme, speaking of the 'alternative, rational and plausible explanation that the disciples stole the body'. The Bishop of Norwich called for Dr Jenkins's resignation. Dr Runcie contented himself with his own Easter sermon in which he stressed that the Resurrection was a 'firm fact' and that the events of it 'were events sure enough'.

In meetings of the General Synod in the autumn of 1984 and the spring of 1985, the archbishop had to face attacks on Dr Jenkins. In November, he dealt with a 'torrid twenty minutes' of questions from the Synod under the glare of television lights. He emphasised that Dr Jenkins's remarks should be seen 'in context', but implied agreement with the view that the way Dr Jenkins had chosen to speak had caused unnecessary hurt to many people. In his Christmas sermon, he implied another criticism, saying that simple people were just as well qualified to understand the message of Christmas as were the learned, and the Christian mystery was not susceptible to logic and reason. His clearest statement of his views came in February 1985 when the Synod debated belief in God. The archbishop said that the work of a bishop involved a 'certain conservative responsibility' – a bishop was a guardian and interpreter of a tradition who should recognise the profound importance of the historic formulas in which the faith was expressed. A bishop, he said, was a bridge-builder, bestriding 'the narrow worlds of mindless dogmatism on the one hand and rootless individualism on the other . . . and,' he added, 'it's a wise bishop who treads with care and reverence'. Further than this, Dr Runcie would not be drawn.

With the miners' strike, Dr Runcie seemed less sure-footed, although equally concerned to steer a middle course. In September 1984, he visited Creswell, a pit in Derbyshire which was working, but where there had been great division over the strike. He was careful to meet miners of all shades of opinion. This act of 'listening' might have been enough for the time being if it had not been for the remarkable Dr Jenkins. At the turn of the month, perhaps chafing at his absence from the headlines for a few weeks, the Bishop of Durham delivered a strong attack, in his first Durham sermon from the pulpit, on government policy during the strike and a personal one on the Coal Board chairman, Ian MacGregor, whom he described as 'an elderly imported American' (Bishop Jenkins is in his 60s, and comes from Croydon). In a slightly strange gesture, Dr Runcie responded by writing a private letter to Ian MacGregor in effect apologising for any offence which might have been caused. The following week, however, Dr Runcie gave an interview to *The Times* in which he appeared to express opinions highly critical of the Government. He told Clifford Longley that if the human consequences of policies aimed at economic growth were too painful 'the objectives must be called into question'; he spoke of the 'efficiency versus compassion argument', and argued that the Church should take the difficult position of moderation – '. . . it is more comfortable to be on the wings than to be clobbered on both sides in the middle'. This interview appeared just before the Conservative Party conference and outraged representatives there who considered it a carefully timed attack. It is doubtful if Dr Runcie intended to be so provocative. Indeed, it is the importance of remaining moderate and middling which seems almost to obsess him. In all his major speeches and sermons, his criticisms of one point of view are always accompanied by soothing

remarks about its strengths. So, for instance, when Dr
Jenkins appeared on television to attack the Government in
March 1985, saying that it should 'risk the defence thing for
the community thing', Dr Runcie's comments were charac-
teristically even-handed. 'Churchmen,' he said, 'should
not pose as naive politicians or amateur economists. But
neither should they be dismissed for raising such fundamental human questions. It is their duty.' Indeed, the
archbishop seems to be increasingly alarmed by what he
believes is the tendency of public argument in Britain to
fall into fiercely opposing camps. He detected a similar
tendency in the General Synod, and warned, in his 'end
of term' speech to the Synod in July 1985 of the danger of
'destructive polarisation, which appears to be becoming
characteristic of our culture'.

The approved phrase to describe Dr Runcie's arch-
bishopric is a 'listening leadership'. There is no doubt that
this works better than a deaf leadership. And it is also true,
as one of the archbishop's former staff points out, that 'you
need myopia to be a visionary' – Dr Runcie is not a visionary
and that makes life at Lambeth Palace easier. If, as most
seem to agree, Dr Runcie is a man who successfully combines many admirable qualities without achieving greatness in the parts or the whole, it is sensible of him not to
aspire to heights which he has no hope of attaining. But the
problem with a policy of 'consolidation' in the Church is
that it assumes that the status quo is sufficiently healthy to
deserve consolidating, and it is not prepared to tell the
harsh truth about so much of the Church's life. Most
bishops, the Archbishop of Canterbury included, feel
that they owe it to Christian charity not to be outspoken in
their criticisms of their own institution. The result, in the
case of the archbishop, is that his considerable amount of
power and huge amount of influence are underused. An
Archbishop of Canterbury can effect profound changes of
mood, even of action, in the Church, as Dr Ramsey showed
with his pushing forward of modernism and centralisation.

Dr Runcie has chosen not to give a comparable lead in the conservative direction which he favours. The Church of England continues to decline, and to separate itself from its members, the people of England, and so if Dr Runcie is consolidating, he is consolidating that decline and that separation.

PART TWO

# THE CLERGY

*by*

*A. N. Wilson*

Archibald Campbell Tait, perhaps the most powerful of the Victorian archbishops of Canterbury, died a little over one hundred years ago in 1882. Before his translation to Canterbury, Tait was Bishop of London, an office which he filled with self-confident Christian dedication. He preached in omnibus yards; he opened Westminster Abbey for evening services (hitherto closed to the public); he nursed cholera victims during the epidemic of 1866; he harried ritualists (in 1858 he suspended the curate of St Barnabas', Pimlico, for hearing confessions); and he regarded with abomination the advance of liberal biblical criticism.

What would Tait have thought, if he could have returned to the Church of England in the 1980s? On Maundy Thursday, 1984, I stood for several hours in St Paul's Cathedral in London, and the vigorous lawn-sleeved ghost of Tait, for some reason, returned persistently to my consciousness. He would certainly have been astonished to discover that his old cathedral church, on this solemn day of the Church's year, had apparently been lent to the Roman Catholics. Doubtless the Romish furnishings of the Cathedral would have raised Tait's astonished eyebrows: the frankly papist baldachino over the High Altar, as well as the gilded mosaics in the dome which so blatantly ape the triumphalist splendours of Italy. But these architectural embellishments would be as nothing, in Tait's eyes, compared with the sight of hundreds of Roman Catholic priests gathered in the transept wearing the coloured stoles which were so specifically forbidden to clergymen of the Protestant obedience. At the altar itself, no less than six bishops stood arrayed in Mass vestments and tall mitres – five of white and one, that of the central figure, of gold. On the rare occasions when this splendid item of headgear was removed, it was revealed that this chief of bishops, this Romish archpriest, was wearing a purple skull-cap. Could it even be . . . ? The shade of Tait trembles at the abomination of desolation: could it even be the Pope himself?

And what is this assembly of Roman Catholic priests doing in St Paul's Cathedral on Maundy Thursday, 1984? They are indulging in what Tait would unquestionably have regarded as the basest form of vulgar superstition. The chief bishop of their assembly is mixing and blessing oils: oil for anointing the sick, oil for smearing on the heads of catechumens, oil of chrism to be used for the consecration of priests and bishops. A little earlier, from the pulpit, this prelate had expounded the mystic meaning of these oils in language which Tait would perhaps have found florid and unmanly. 'The oil of chrism', he had said, 'is not just olive oil. Into it is poured the oil of flowers from which arises a glorious fragrance': a fragrance which he found symbolic of the sacerdotal ministry. After this sermon, the priests had all arisen and renewed their ordination vows. The bishop said: 'My brothers, this day we celebrate the memory of the first Eucharist, when our Lord appointed his apostles to go forth and bear fruit in his name, so calling them and us to serve him in a royal priesthood of his Church . . .' And afterwards they all vowed to renew their dedication to Christ 'as ministers of the new covenant'.

When the ghost of Tait had recovered from the sight of the strange prelate in a mitre, he might possibly have found much in these definitions of priesthood to match his own demanding views. He would surely have found little objectionable in the modern pontiff's question, 'Are you determined to imitate Christ Jesus our Saviour, who is head of the Church and chief shepherd of the flock, by teaching faithfully those truths which he received from his Father, and by a selfless concern for the people committed to your care?' It was just such a commitment which Tait, when

Bishop of London, looked for in his clergy, though he would probably also wish to add that he expected them to be gentlemen.

He would therefore surely have blinked a little as the priests took their seats and there appeared to arise beneath the dome of Saint Paul's a gaggle of extremely effeminate clergy, clad more simply than the rest in dark blue cassocks. Many of them wore spectacles. Some had long hair bound up in buns or what to Tait's Victorian eyes would look like chignons. And these too – these castrati or temple eunuchs – in their high piping voices are promising to rededicate themselves 'to that office in the Church to which God has called you'.

It is now time to tell Archbishop Tait the truth and to break the news to him as gently as we can. These figures in dark blue cassocks are actually women. They are deaconesses. Although High churchmen are battling fiercely to maintain the distinction between deacons and deaconesses, and to point out that so-called deaconesses are *not* admitted to the Order of Deacons, it is a distinction which is inevitably blurred in the minds of laymen. Many bishops now 'ordain' deacons and deaconesses indiscriminately at the same ceremony. In provinces of the Anglican Communion abroad – Hong Kong, the United States, New Zealand and elsewhere – women have even been ordained to the priesthood.

The ghost of Tait has grown pale. Are we trying to tell him that these females, fantastically arrayed in Saint Paul's Cathedral, are members of the Church of England by law established? We are. But what of these papistically-clad priests? What of the bishops in their tall mitres? They, too, every man of them, belong to the Church of England. Even quite 'moderate' churchmen among them practise forms of devotion which would, by the terms of the Public Worship Regulation Act of 1874, be illegal. It is not merely that a large proportion of churches in London are High Church – with vestments, the reservation of the Blessed Sacrament,

regular times for confession, and daily or frequent celebrations of the Eucharist. It is that the 'moderates' and even
many of the Low Church clergy regard as normal practice
things which Tait regarded as the very height of papistical
superstition.

When he has absorbed the fact that the assembly in St
Paul's is a gathering of the clergy – priests, deacons and
deaconesses of the diocese of London – we shall perhaps
leave him to work out for himself the fact that the figure in
their midst, blessing oils and preaching a sermon about the
sweet fragrance of sacerdotal consecration, is none other
than Tait's successor, the Bishop of London himself, the Rt
Rev and Rt Hon Graham Leonard.

External fashions in religious, as in secular costume
change. But there are lessons to be learnt about the violent
differences in outward manner, appearance, custom, and
(seemingly) belief between the late Victorian Dr Tait and
the mid-Elizabethan Dr Leonard. And among all the questions raised by these differences, none is more sharply
marked than the question of holy orders. Dr Leonard began
his homily on that Maundy Thursday by asking the question, 'What are priests for?' and it is quite largely the extent
to which it has found different answers to this question in
different generations which has shaped the evolution of the
English Church.

*   *   *

Before asking, with Dr Leonard, *What are priests for?* it might
be helpful to ask the simpler, but more difficult, question,
*What are priests?* It is a question from which others follow
such as: Does the Church of England mean by the word
priest what it always meant? Does it mean by the word
priest what other churches mean by it?

The Epistle to the Hebrews makes it plain that the temple
priesthood of the Jews has been replaced, in the new
dispensation, by the single, perfect and complete priesthood of Christ. The old high priests made sacrifices first for

their own sins and then for those of the people. Christ, who was the perfect high priest, did not need to sacrifice for his own sin – for he was sinless – nor does he, like the Levitical priests, need to repeat his sacrifice. For he sprinkled and purified the people not with the blood of goats and heifers, but with his own precious blood.

> All the priests stand at their duties every day, offering over and over again the same sacrifices which are quite incapable of taking sins away. He, on the other hand, has offered one single sacrifice for sins, and then taken his place for ever, at the right hand of God (Heb. 10:11,12 Jerusalem Bible).

Priesthood in the Christian dispensation is something which belongs to Christ alone and in the New Testament, the words priest and priesthood (*Hiereus* and *Hierateuma*) are only applied collectively to the Christian people (1 Pet. 2:5, Rev. 5:10) never to the Christian ministers, who are the elders (*presbuteroi*) and deacons (*diakonoi*). The elders are sometimes referred to as bishops (*episkopoi*) and in the early years of the Church it would seem that there was no order of priesthood as such, separate from that of the episcopate. Indeed, it is only by the end of the second century that we first read of Christian ministers being called *priests* and in these cases it is not always clear whether the elders or bishops are referred to.

Saint Cyprian, who was martyred as Bishop of Carthage in 258, wrote of *sacerdotes*, priestly ministers who shared in the episcopal priesthood, by which it would appear he meant (the reference is to be found in his 61st Epistle) that the priests could, with the bishop's dispensation, preside at the Eucharist and lay forgiving hands on penitents. Even 150 years later, a letter of Pope Innocent I (AD 416) made it plain that ministers who offered the Eucharist in country districts far from a bishop only did so on the bishop's behalf. Thus a priest, making the offering at the altar or pronouncing God's forgiveness for the sins of the penitent, is a man acting on behalf of his elder or bishop; and the bishop is a man who is merely exercising on earth the one, perfect and indivisible priesthood of Christ. When Christians speak of their *priests* they are using shorthand.

In spite of the increased 'sacerdotalism' of the Western church during the Middle Ages, and in spite of the gradual development of the 'threefold order' of the Catholic Church (bishops, priests, and deacons) there was no diminution in the sense of priests being men who exercised their ministry under obedience to, and on behalf of, their bishop. With the development of the power and importance of the Holy See, it was also seen that the bishops themselves exercised their authority under obedience to the Vicar of Christ, a Western attitude which was, of course, abhorrent to Eastern Churches whose allegiance was to various other patriarchates. The crisis in the English Church during the reign of Henry VIII, therefore, hinged upon the obedience of laity and ministers to bishops, and the obedience of bishops to Rome, rather than on any quasi-magical 'validity' of the priest's orders themselves.

After the cataclysms of Henry VIII's reign, when the Church of England began to form and reform itself and when the first Prayer Book of Edward VI was drawn up in 1549, it retained the ancient, Catholic and threefold order of bishops, priests and deacons, as did the second Prayer Book of 1552. But for that generation of Christians, questions of law and of polity were much more important than questions of sacramental validity. This can be shown in the events, both of the next reign of Queen Mary and those of her sister, Elizabeth. In Mary's reign, when Reginald Pole finally reached England, he did not insist upon the reordination of those who had been priested by the illegal, Protestant Edwardian ordinal. Only in some dozen cases was this ceremony gone through during Mary's reign, compared with hundreds of ordinations which must have taken place in Edward's reign. All that concerned Pole was to undo the state of schism into which the Reformation had plunged England.

Elizabeth I self-confidently led the Church of England back into schism, but once again, in her settlement, retained the threefold Catholic order. Her chief theologian and defender, Richard Hooker, did not, however, consider the episcopate as necessary, merely as convenient. It was his belief that the episcopate was of the *bonum esse*, not of the *esse* of a church. Whether the Church of England is essentially episcopal, or primarily a national institution, has been often debated, of course, in modern times during the course of discussions about disestablishment, as well as in the ecumenical overtures between Anglicans and the other Protestant sectaries. It was only in the early years of James I's reign that C. Holywood, SJ, began to put about the notion that Anglican orders were not 'valid'; that is, that Anglican priests did not have the power to forgive sins or the right to preside at the Eucharistic offering. He claimed, in a story which has since been shown to be the purest fabrication, that Elizabeth I's Archbishop of Canterbury, Matthew Parker, was not properly consecrated, but took his consecration vows in a semi-drunken fashion at the Nag's Head tavern in Cheapside. At the time of Parker's consecration, no Roman Catholic expressed doubt as to its validity. What was in doubt was its lawfulness.

The obsession with validity, however, took on new intensity in the nineteenth century, both among the clergy of the Established Church and among the Romanist propagandists. By then, it must be doubted whether many English bishops would have wished to claim for themselves the full powers of a Catholic prelate, nor whether many of the parsons in the Church of England believed, as they knelt at the north end of their holy tables, that they were transforming bread and wine into the body and blood of Christ; still less whether they would have viewed the priest's power of absolution in the confessional as anything other than a gross and heretical piece of pretended magic.

Those who did believe in the full Catholic validity of
Anglican orders had, in the early years of the nineteenth
century, as much difficulty in persuading the hierarchy of
the English as of the Roman Church that this doctrine was
true. No more optimistic promulgators of the teaching
could be found than the members of the Order of Corporate
Reunion, a body of priests who, in the 1870s, believed that
if all Anglican clergymen could be persuaded to accept
conditional reordination, the Church of Rome would be
only too happy to embrace the Church of England back into
the one true fold of the Redeemer. With this end in view,
the Vicar of All Saints', Lambeth, the Rev Dr Frederick
Reginald Benedict Lee, together with two other clergymen
by the names of Moss and Seccombe, took part in a
strikingly ecumenical rite in the summer of 1877. In a boat
at Murano, near Venice, these three Anglican priests
were conditionally rebaptised, confirmed, made deacon,
ordained priest and consecrated bishops all in the space of
the same afternoon and on board the same boat. Who the
consecrating prelates were on this occasion has never been
fully determined, but it is said that there were three bishops
involved, one Greek Orthodox, one Copt and one Roman
Catholic. At home in England, the three newly consecrated
bishops lost no time in performing secret reordinations
upon their Anglican brethren in an effort to make certain of
the validity of Anglican orders. Dr Lee was perhaps the
most eccentric of the three, and his exotic rites at All Saints',
Lambeth, became in their day popular. As was said by a
Roman Catholic priest at the time, 'Lee was undoubtedly a
Bishop, which is more than can be said of his neighbour at
Lambeth Palace'.[1]

The *episcopi vagantes* form a colourful sideshow to
nineteenth- and twentieth-century Church history, being
walking embodiments of the antithesis of Hooker's view of
the episcopal function. Hooker thought it was technically,
theologically, possible to think of a church without bishops.
He had never dreamed of the fantastic possibility of a

bishop without a church. Their existence reflects, one would think, an extraordinarily mechanical view of the sacraments of holy orders. But it is a view which was by no means discouraged by the encyclical *Apostolicae Curae*, promulgated by Leo XIII in 1896, which pronounced Anglican Orders 'absolutely null and void', through defect of form and intention. This Bull has not been revoked at the time of writing, but there begin to be signs of a change of heart in Rome about the matter.

Most Roman Catholics in England today would be prepared to recognise that *Apostolicae Curae* was mistaken both on theological and on historical grounds. The recent ecumenical statements of ARCIC (the Anglican Roman Catholic International Commission) make it plain that the theologicans of the two churches in fact have very similar views of the sacred ministry,[2] and that there is mutual recognition between the two churches. In modern times, in spite of the caution with which the English Roman Catholic hierarchy view the Church of England, there has been warm acceptance of Anglicans in Europe; travelling Anglican priests are allowed to celebrate the Eucharist at Spanish and French altars. But, in historical terms, *Apostolicae Curae* was of the greatest importance. It prompted, from the Archbishops of Canterbury and York, a response (Answer to the Apostolic Letter of Pope Leo XIII) which made it *unambiguously* clear that they claimed for the priesthood and episcopate of the English Church the same powers and authority as those of Rome. Most theological definitions in history have come about as a result of conflict. It is almost unimaginable that the Archbishops of York and Canterbury, in the earlier part of the nineteenth century, would have issued what amounts to an encyclical, insisting on the power of English priests to pronounce the absolution of sins and to offer 'sacrifice in the Church for the living and the dead'. Where diffidence, indifference or positive hostility to the rebellious temper of high churchmen had, in the early nineteenth century, made the Church of England keep silent, chauvinism and xenophobia drew out of it a fullness of Catholic claims which were to define its view of priesthood for the next ninety years. There would probably be still as many views of priesthood in the Church of England as there were priests. But it had now been made clear to the world that the Anglican ordinal was no mere form of words, and that those made bishop, priest or deacon according to its formularies were just as 'validly' ordained or consecrated as Bishop Lee of Lambeth, or Leo XIII himself.

The surprising thing, when one looks back upon the passions aroused by *Apostolicae Curae*, was that the Pope chose to assault the national church in that particular way, and to attack an ordinal which subsequent theological investigation has shown to be no less valid than any other of Catholic Christendom. For the original objection to the Church of England, by Reginald Pole and his contemporaries, remains the one which continues to trouble all the ecumenists. In the old ordinal of the Book of Common Prayer, the bishop says to each ordinand in turn: 'Receive the Holy Ghost for office and work of a Priest in the Church of God.' But, if our earlier definition of priesthood – as a purely vicarious function – is a correct one, it is still difficult to see how one can speak of a Church exercising priesthood while living in schism from the rest of Christendom. For a bishop receives his authority and power from Christ alone, and the priest only exercises the priestly functions on the bishop's behalf. While a church remains in schism (as a national church such as the Church of England must, by definition, be) there must be something imperfect about its priesthood; or, at the very least, vague about its understanding of priesthood.

In the current debate, for example, about whether or not women should be ordained to the priesthood, the issue has proved divisive on purely ecumenical lines. Many of the reasons put forward against ordaining women to the priesthood are probably about as rational as arguments against

admitting women to a London club. But among this chaos
of prejudice there runs a hard core of ecumenical understanding. If the Church of England believes that it has
priesthood, then this priesthood does not *belong* to it any
more than any of the sacraments can *belong* to any one
branch of the Catholic Church. So the argument runs.
We all partake of the priesthood of Christ. There is not
such a thing as Church of England priesthood or Roman
Catholic priesthood: merely the priesthood of Jesus
Christ. One cannot make a fundamental change in sacramental custom while continuing to say that one wishes
to labour to undo the schism and division of the centuries. If we share priesthood with the Orthodox and the
Roman Catholics, then (the argument runs) we must all
wait *together* until the moment when we all wish to ordain
women.

Since there is about as much chance of the Greek Orthodox Church ordaining women to the priesthood as there is
of their deciding to acquire their own nuclear deterrent, the
argument is thought by many to be a little dishonest. If it is
right to ordain women, they say, we should do so, and not
hold back merely in order to please members of 'other
churches'. Many surprising members of 'other churches',
such as Mother Teresa of Calcutta, are in any case in favour
of ordaining women. But the argument throws an interesting light on the differences of viewpoint in the national
Church about orders and about Church Order. For even to
speak of 'other churches' implies a theology of the Church
which is much at variance with the professed catholicism of
many ecumenical pronouncements.

Perhaps, in pastoral, as opposed to theological, terms,
none of this matters very much. Keble, when troubled by
the heresies or follies of his fellow Anglicans, was wont to
say that as far as he was concerned 'the Church' was his
parish. A later saint of the English Church, Father Andrew,
of the Society of the Divine Compassion, put the matter
more devastatingly when he wrote to advise someone who

felt that they had lost their faith in the 'validity' of Anglican orders:

> In approaching this matter the whole point really is, what kind of God do you believe in? When a priest goes to the altar is it a case of the priest using God to bring the Sacrament to the altar, or God using the priest to give His sacrament to the people?[3]

Thus, whatever the unsatisfactoriness of Anglican polity, members of the Church of England can believe that their priests dispense the priesthood of Jesus Christ. This does not diminish the importance of such discussions as those of the Anglican-Roman Catholic International Commission, nor the ecumenical dialogues with the Orthodox, nor those with other Protestant churches. Because 'the communion of the churches in mission, faith and holiness . . . is symbolised and maintained in the bishop'[4] there is something gravely lacking in a church whose bishops are in schism with the greater part of Christendom. But because Jesus Christ is fully present in his sacraments in the English as in the Russian, Greek or Roman churches, there is a more important sense in which nothing is lacking. This is another way of saying about the Church of England that in so far as it is a divine society, its adherents are 'very members incorporate in the mystical body of [God's] Son' and its priests ministers of his grace. But in so far as it is a human organisation it is very conspicuously less than perfect and its ministers share in, when they do not actively embody, this imperfection. The twenty-sixth of the thirty-nine articles speaks of 'the unworthiness of Ministers which hinders not the effect of the Sacrament'. It further goes on to say that 'inquiry should be made of evil Ministers, and that they be accused by those that have knowledge of their offences'. It is not the purpose of this chapter to concentrate upon the evil ministers. But it is to the human beings who are called to the sacred ministry in the Church of England that attention must now turn.

And first of all, *called*. Anglicans do not, as a whole, grow up with the same sense of 'vocation' as is instilled, or used to be, in the bosoms of young Roman Catholics. It is unlikely that the *Church Times* would ever carry a headline such as the startling, not to say eerie, news in the *Catholic Herald* April 27th, 1984, 'VOCATIONS GALORE AT PLYMOUTH'. Nor is it entirely imaginable how the Anglican authorities would cope with such an eventuality were it to occur within the bosom of the Established Church.

Nevertheless, there are at any time quite considerable numbers of men (and growing numbers of women) who feel called to the priesthood in the Church of England. This feeling of 'calling' differs strongly from case to case. To compare the oral testimonies of those who have felt it is to encounter figures as different as Trollope's Archdeacon Grantly and the prophet Amos. Mr Y, the son and grandson of a clergyman, had assumed that he wanted to be an architect, but during his first year at university began to wonder whether he should not be ordained. He took the somewhat unusual step of talking about it directly to a bishop who took the even more unusual step of saying, 'Let's assume it is a true vocation from God unless we are told to the contrary.' Mr Y's experience was one of a gradual unfolding of what 'seemed right', and his description of how he came to be in holy orders does not differ markedly from descriptions one has heard of how people came to be solicitors or to follow their father into the family firm. Mr X, however, was an atheist who had never had any dealings with the Christian religion. He worked as an apprentice journalist on a weekly paper. To judge from a sermon which he preached in the hearing of the authors of this book, he had a conversion experience every bit as dramatic as that of the apostle Paul. At one minute he was an indifferent worldling. At the next, he was burning with a love of Christ and – a feeling which developed almost simultaneously – the knowledge that he must serve Christ as a clergyman of the Church of England. Between these two extremes of gradual decision to 'become a clergyman' and violent 'calling' there must be as many gradations of feeling and emotion as there are those who have had the experience.

Until the Second World War those who had such feelings – or had no feelings at all but had merely decided that they would like to occupy one of the many handsome parsonages then so plentifully available for priests of the Church of England and their families – had only to satisfy the bishop's examining chaplain that they were not wholly insane or illiterate. Often enough, the candidate never saw a bishop until the day of his ordination. He usually spent some time at one of the theological colleges, but his decision to go or remain there was a matter between himself and the college principal.

Everything is different now. At the end of the Second World War, large numbers of men emerged from the forces with the idea of becoming parsons and the Church of England responded by setting up a body known as CACTM, whose methods were based on those of officer selection conferences in the army. CACTM later changed its name to ACCM (the Advisory Council for the Church's Ministry), but its methods of selection have not differed markedly, though perhaps they now owe less to the military and more to the Civil Service who eliminate those candidates who fail to make a decent impression at their notorious 'weekends'.

The procedure to be followed by any person who feels called to the sacred ministry of the Church of England now follows these lines. An interview is arranged with the Director of Ordinands (DDO) in the diocese where the recipient of the divine call happens to reside. This director is a clergyman, usually with other calls on his time and in most cases, though by no means all, with a parish of his own to run. It can therefore take months to arrange an interview with the DDO as he is called. (The Church of England shares with the army a passion for initials. Or, as we might say, in the C of E you go to the DDO to see if you are suitable to be sent to an ACCM conference.) When the interview has been arranged, the DDO will assess, from your age, professional or academic background and general demeanour, whether you are obviously unsuitable. If he decides that you *are*, you have no redress and will have to go to another diocese and start the whole procedure again. One layman, with a clean record medically and psychologically, and who has never been in trouble with the police, has been told (he informs the authors of this book) by the DDOs of two dioceses that they are not prepared to send him to a selection conference. Perhaps there are others who share his plight.

If, however, you *are* sent to a selection conference, a lot of preliminary investigation into your good character will be set in motion. The candidate himself must fill in a form giving a frank medical history of himself, and answer a long questionnaire which includes such inquiries as, 'Are you afraid of the dark?' 'Do you have or have you at any stage had a bedwetting problem?' and finally, 'Have you lost interest in almost everything?' He must also submit to an independent medical examination by a doctor engaged by ACCM and present a wide range of referees, including the names of his employer, his parish priest and a lay person who knows him well. It is unlikely that anyone under the age of 18 or over the age of 70 will be subjected to these rigorous enquiries, but some exceptions have been known.

When your documents are all in order, you will be summoned to a selection conference, usually held in some diocesan retreat house far from where you live. About twenty or thirty candidates are usually involved in this exercise, and they will be placed under the scrutiny of a panel of selectors for a period of about three days. The panel is made up of a senior, but not ludicrously senior, cleric (a dean or a suffragan bishop would be normal) who is the chairman; someone designed to test your intellectual suitability (this might be a lecturer at a training college, but not necessarily); someone whose job is to assess your *pastoral* gifts (in the old days this would probably have been an experienced parish priest, but the tendency now is, if possible, to get a deaconess, a female parish helper, or indeed anyone who is a woman); and finally a lay person, again, if at all possible, a woman.

The disadvantage of this system is precisely the same as that which threatens the workability of the jury service in our courts. Those with sound judgment are on the whole those who have, if at all possible, extricated themselves from fulfilling this role. They believe themselves to have 'better things to do with their time'. The selectors at such conferences are therefore either competent people in a hurry to get back to their normal avocations, or people with nothing better to do whose instincts about human character are not always to be esteemed very highly.

Each ACCM conference follows exactly the same form. On the first evening of their arrival, the candidates and the selectors all sit round in a semicircle and are obliged to spend two minutes saying a few words about themselves. This excruciating exercise is designed to 'break the ice'. Some people gabble a few words of half-prepared curriculum vitae giving details of education, employment or progeny, while others use the two minutes as an opportunity to testify to the moment when the Lord called them from factory floor or office stool to serve him in the ministry. At the end of two minutes the handbell is ruthlessly rung and it is the turn of the next person.

Candidates then troop into chapel where a more-or-less standard sermon is preached by the chairman of the selectors. He tells them that we have all been called by God to work for his Kingdom, but that some of us, alas, have not been called to the sacred ministry. At the end of the three days, when the selectors have convened, they will tell some candidates that they have been recommended for training. In some cases they are recommended unconditionally, in others only if certain conditions are fulfilled (such as their taking some A-levels or having some particular experience of life in the world: factory work used to be very popular). Some candidates will be told that they have *not yet* been recommended. They should try again at some future date. Perhaps they are too young; or perhaps their circumstances of life do not make it possible for them, at the moment, to undergo full-time training at a theological college. Other candidates will be told that they are not recommended, but that 'the candidate should explore other spheres of service to find his vocation'. They then, having been given this rather depressing warning, arise and sing some such hymn as 'Just as I am, without one plea', or 'God moves in a mysterious way His wonders to perform'.

It is worth while pointing out at this juncture that the Church of England could not possibly afford to train all the candidates who come forward to join the ranks of the sacred ministry; and that, even if they could afford to train them, they could not afford to employ them in the parochial system, to house them, their wives and their children, nor even pay them the meagre pensions allotted to parsons when they retire. In other words, if there were (as in the *Catholic Herald* headline) 'VOCATIONS GALORE IN PLYMOUTH' this would spell financial ruin for the Anglican bishop of the area. And it is the job of the selectors at ACCM conferences not to recommend more candidates for training than the bishops can afford to maintain. Each candidate is sponsored by a diocesan bishop and he remains that bishop's legal and financial responsibility until he disgraces himself or chooses to leave the bishop's diocese. The working of the Holy Ghost has, therefore, to be kept very vigorously under control in order to avoid the diocese going 'into the red'.

In the course of the three days, the candidates occupy themselves by conducting discussion groups. An idea is allowed to float about that these groups are an important part of the selection procedure. Subjects under discussion range from contemporary crises in industry to questions such as 'mission'. The bossier members of each group take charge; the shy ones say little; most people guilelessly try to make 'contributions' to the discussion which will prove them to be worthy of ordination. But these discussions are, from that point of view, fairly pointless since they are only rarely supervised by any of the selectors. The main point of the discussion groups is to keep everyone occupied while individual private interviews are being conducted.

Each candidate has a private interview with each of the selectors, and at the end of the three days, the selectors convene to decide which candidates must be discarded. ACCM tacitly insists that some candidates *are* discarded each time for the financial reasons already stated.

Many of those who have attended a number of ACCM conferences, either as observers, candidates or selectors, must have had their faith tried if they were under the impression that the final selections were the result of guidance by the Holy Spirit. Anyone involved in the process must have known perfectly good men who were 'turned down by ACCM' for no decent reason. Equally, some of the candidates chosen as suitable have been, to say the least, bizarre. It is obviously a ridiculous method of selecting suitable ordinands: highly wasteful of time, money and emotion.

* * *

The successful candidates must begin their ordination training, and this usually starts on the earliest autumn after the ACCM conference. Certain ill-educated candidates (for example, no A-levels) might be obliged to undertake the Aston Training Scheme, a part-time 'foundation course' on the Open University pattern. But all this would be simply in order to get them to the position of the other ordinands who are sent to train at theological colleges.

Nowadays we take it as axiomatic that 'professional qualifications' are required in almost all jobs. Figures who, in the past, would simply learn their craft as they went along – like teachers or cooks – now go to 'college'. One therefore assumes that there is something perfectly natural about having training-colleges for clergymen. In fact, the theological colleges of the Church of England developed for very unmodern and, it would now seem, peculiar reasons. When Sydney Smith took deacon's orders in 1794, all that was required of him by the bishop's examining chaplain was that he should be able to construe certain passages of the New Testament in Greek, a work which he had spent the previous summer perusing with no evident enthusiasm. As it turned out, Smith was (in addition to being the greatest wit of his age) a diligent parish priest, but he learnt nothing of his preaching technique, his sick visiting, his instruction of catechumens, his care for the fabric of old buildings, when he was 'preparing for the ministry'. Nor did many other men ordained to the sacred ministry over the next hundred years. But by the close of the nineteenth century, the Tractarians had made their distinctive influence felt in further quarters of the Established Church than the merely 'high'. A place such as Cuddesdon, a windswept hill an inconvenient distance from Oxford, was the perfect site for a large Gothic edifice, designed by George Edmund Street, in which to respond to our Lord's call to personal holiness.

This was its function when the saintly Edward King was its first principal (later Bishop of Lincoln) and this was the function of many of the early theological colleges. (Chichester was the first; founded in 1838.) Men were not sent there to learn theology. They had already learnt that at universities. They were not sent there to learn about pastoral care or parish life; they learnt that on the ground during their first years as curates. They were sent there to learn prayer and personal holiness. This was the point of Cuddesdon, Chichester, Salisbury, Wells, Ely, and the various other Tractarian colleges. Men sometimes went there for a year, sometimes for a month or two. But their function was purely spiritual.

Mr Wopsle, the parish clerk in *Great Expectations* (whose

performance of Hamlet forms such a notable scene in the novel) was fond of saying what would happen if the Church was 'thrown open'. ('If you could only give him his head, he would read the clergyman into fits.') Wopsle never lived to see the Church thrown open, but once it was, it became necessary to open colleges to provide intellectual as well as spiritual education. The monks of Kelham and the priests at Warminster provided at their theological colleges (both now defunct) a pattern of education directly modelled on that of continental seminaries, designed for non-graduates.

Needless to say, the High Church flavour of the colleges mentioned provoked reactions of various tempers. Ridley Hall in Cambridge, Wycliffe Hall in Oxford or Oak Hill in Barnet were founded with the specific purpose of training Evangelical or low church clergymen, while Ripon Hall at Oxford began with the intention of turning out 'modern' or 'broad' churchmen. It would come as some surprise to Christians of other traditions (Baptists, for instance, or Roman Catholics) to discover that the theological colleges are, to this day, purely freelance institutions. There is no 'official' method of training the clergy in the Church of England, though since the development of ACCM in power and size a closer watch is kept on the theological colleges than was once the case. They are autonomous institutions, ruled by their own governing bodies, presided over by their own principals and staff and still surprisingly proud (considering the disastrous effect of divisions and parties within the Church) of their own distinctive 'traditions'. This is perhaps truer of the 'high' colleges than of the 'low' ones. At St Stephen's House in Oxford, for instance, students are still sniggered at if they do not wear precisely the 'correct' cut of cassock. Small hope there for a Christian of a faintly different Anglican tradition ('middle stump', say, or Evangelical) of feeling much at home.

The candidates will, therefore, almost certainly drift towards a college which 'suits' them, and few bishops would bother to stop them. An exception is Graham Leonard, the extremely Anglo-Catholic Bishop of London, who encourages candidates from his diocese to attend Oak Hill theological college, a place of firmly Protestant tradition. This is because both the college and the bishop recognise that what they hold in common is far stronger and richer than the superficial externals which divide them. Oak Hill has also been noted for its contribution to ecumenical endeavours. For instance, when a group of Greek Orthodox priests and seminarians asked the Archbishop of Canterbury if they could spend a term at an Anglican theological college, many people were astonished that Dr Runcie selected Oak Hill as the place they should attend. The reasons were largely geographical (proximity to London, the ability to accommodate the Greek party, etc.), but the experiment worked well. The Orthodox were impressed by the vigour of the biblical Christianity, the depth of spirituality and the strength of learning that they found there.

When a candidate goes to a theological college, what does he learn there? Methods of training, and the idiosyncrasies of individual tutors and lecturers, are changing all the time so it would be dangerous to generalise. The general purpose of all the theological colleges, however, is obvious. On the one hand, each candidate is meant to be trained in basic theological learning before his ordination. For this they are required to pass a thing called the general ordination examination (shortened, inevitably, to GOE) which consists of six general subjects: Holy Scripture, Christian doctrine, Church history, Christian worship, Christian ethics, pastoral studies. It has to be said that, although this all sounds very impressive, none of these subjects is studied in depth and no very exacting standard is applied by the examiners.

In addition, of course, the colleges are meant to provide practical training in what the 'higher' establishments call 'priestcraft'. It used to be said that the 'higher' church colleges produced a more 'professional' type of clergyman.

Candidates at Chichester and at St Stephen's House, Oxford, are still, for instance, *taught* such obviously useful things as how to approach an undertaker on someone else's behalf when a parishioner dies; what is expected of a clergyman during a sick visit, or during a visit to a house of bereaved persons. On the other hand, it has to be admitted that other once-'high' colleges like Ripon College, Cuddesdon, do not necessarily keep up this degree of professionalism. During the years 1970–6 no student at Cuddesdon was taught how to baptise a baby.

Apart from lessons in pastoralia or priestcraft (How do you hear a confession? What do you do if someone rings up and asks for their house to be exorcised? How do you run a parish school?), each student is expected, with a word borrowed from the social workers, to have a 'placement' during his period of training. This means that they attach themselves to a local hospital, prison, school or parish and try to learn some of the practical skills which will be required of them when they begin their ministry. Obviously, some of these 'placements' are of more use than others. In some places, students opt for the cushiest possible task ('I serve Mass twice a week for some nuns' was one ordinand's 'placement') while others wear themselves out doing worthy things at, say, the local borstal, but still remain unprepared for the shock of walking for the first time into a geriatric ward (something all parochial clergy have to do very frequently, or should do).

We have mentioned intellectual and professional training. It is clear, however, in the minds of those who preside over ACCM that theological colleges exercise a third function which it is less easy to justify, or to define. Before attempting to do so, a quotation might be helpful – from a parish newsletter picked up from the back of a church in London. The author is a deaconess who has recently completed her training:

For the sake of the Kingdom I was prepared to polish my Greek and my image. The trouble is, Theological College is also a place where images get shattered as well as polished . . . Theological education is – or should be – a violent process. It means – or should mean – transformation. It is hard to see any other reason why we need it.

The article is unsigned. It is merely, we are told, 'from the deaconess'. The article as a whole makes it clear that being at theological college was purgatorial, and that there had been a deliberate policy, on the part of the authorities, of breaking the candidates down. In a large number of colleges, the techniques of the modern lunatic asylum are borrowed, and there are 'group sharing sessions'. For those unfamiliar with these groups, it is perhaps necessary to explain that a number of people sit round in a circle and tell the 'truth' about each other. It is often an opportunity for hurling abuse at people you dislike. People emerge from these sessions either purified, as the deaconess says she was purified, or emotionally shattered, which often comes to the same thing. Some people doubtless emerge from theological colleges with a sturdier degree of self-knowledge. Others emerge as self-obsessed, psychological wrecks.

Even in cases where this state of crisis is not deliberately fostered by techniques borrowed from the psychoanalysts, the 'strain' of theological college life is something to which most students would bear witness. It may be that no part of the training – pastoral, intellectual, spiritual – is done to a high level. But it is all done in bits, so that the theological student's day (contrasted with that of an ordinary undergraduate's, say) is one rush from chapel to meal, to lecture room, to 'placement'. The background of this hectic routine is a community which is often extremely inward-looking. In a hot-house it is the orchidaceous blooms which flourish. Many students give up not because they have 'lost their faith' or because they do not believe that God is calling them

to the sacred ministry, but because they cannot stomach the
atmosphere of theological college life.

In spite of the obvious disadvantages of the system, all
the bishops of the Church of England have now made a
gentleman's agreement among themselves that they will
stick to certain 'guidelines' laid down by ACCM. They will
not ordain anyone under the age of 29 unless he has spent
three years at a fully-residential theological college. Those
over 30 (there are now many such candidates) must spend a
minimum of two years in this way. One might echo, loudly
and with vigour, the deaconess's question: *'It is hard to see
any reason why we need it.'*[5]

\* \* \*

The student's last year at theological college is dominated
by the search for a job. This, again, would probably puzzle
Christians of other traditions. If you have given yourself to
the service of God in his Church, and accepted the patronage of a bishop, you will surely go where you are sent and
do what is asked of you? But this is not the case. The
situation is further complicated by the fact that your employer, when you become a curate, or a deaconess working
in a parish, is not the bishop but, in effect, the parish priest.
Thus, while the newly-fledged deacon or deaconess is
anxious to get a church which 'suits' them, and certain
parish priests might be desperate for curates and helpers,
these two sets of desires might rarely coincide. And neither
desire is worth anything if money is not forthcoming from
the diocese or from some other supplementary source such
as the Additional Curates' Society. Thus, the last year at
theological college, apart from the ordinary purgatory of
college routines, adds to the ordinand the strain of many
conflicting needs, worries and demands. If he is a married
man, or even if he is a bachelor with strong family ties,
parents and so forth, he will inevitably want a parish which
suits his domestic routines. He will also, very likely, be
looking for a particular type of church. An ardent young

Evangelical fresh from, let us say, St John's College, Nottingham, or Oak Hill, will certainly be on the lookout for a 'lively' parish, with many outlets and opportunities for mission. Similarly, a seminarian from Chichester or St Stephen's House, Oxford, *plus catholique que le pape* will be seeking diligently for a church which has, at least, Reservation of the Blessed Sacrament, frequent if not daily celebrations, set times for confession, vestments, incense and, on Sundays, a sung celebration. Traditionalists will even be in search of vicars who still 'have' Benediction.

These considerations, in the case of the majority of theological students, have to be modified. It is only the lucky few who get 'exactly what they want' in their first curacy; and one may question the Christian efficacy of a church whose ministers use such language – as the majority do – about their first cure of souls. Most will also be aware, however, that their period of training has so far been at best imperfect, at worst wholly and woefully inadequate, and they will look to their first employers to teach them in the ways of priestcraft. Being a priest, or for that matter being a deacon or a deaconess, if it is learnt at all, is learnt by practice, and most of the clergy who feel that they are in the right profession would say that they owed much to their first vicar.

The situation, however, is by no means so satisfactory as it once was. The curate, that standard figure of fun in so much of English literature and comic lore, was once a very common figure; he is now a rarity. This is partly because the Church of England has been hit by the economic changes of the 1960s–80s. But it is also because she now chooses to spend her money on different things, and partly because curates have become greedier. Before the war, it was not uncommon to pay a curate £100 *per annum*: not a princely sum, even when allowances have been made for inflation. A curate did not expect to drive a car, or have central heating, or, really, to be married. He recognised that he had given himself up to God's service and if he wished to enjoy these luxuries, he felt he had to wait for them. Now, with men getting ordained aged 45, the fathers of children already at school, or with a widowed mother-in-law to 'help' and a wife who does not wish to give up her job as a solicitor, the whole picture has changed radically. Such people cannot be pushed around in the way that the young unmarried curates used to be. Also, it has to be said that the Church is not willing (or able) to pay for curates where they are not needed. Sparsely attended churches in, say, Bethnal Green, during the 1920s or 1930s would invariably have one or two – perhaps three or four – ill-paid curates, because the diocese of London would have thought it worth paying £100 a year each towards this expenditure. Now, with most dioceses paying a large 'quota' to the General Synod, and with an expensive administrative machine to keep in order (the diocese of Oxford employs as many secretaries as it does curates) it is felt that there is less money to spare for the clergy.

Against this background, it is perhaps hardly surprising that newly-ordained deacons do not always land themselves with jobs in a parish where the vicar is an ideal priest-maker. The reason he has asked for a curate, almost certainly, is that he has a large parish and feels overworked himself. He will want the curate to relieve him of work, not to provide extra work by needing advice, admonition and assistance. Many of those who would be best at giving this advice, or who would make ideal employers by the force of their examples, live and work in parishes which, for one reason or another, the diocese would not dream of supplying with a curate.

The Alternative Service Book tells us that 'A deacon is called to serve the Church of God, and to work with its members in caring for the poor, the needy, the sick, and all who are in trouble. He is to strengthen the faithful, search out the careless and indifferent, and to preach the word of God in the place to which he is licensed.' Presumably, the function of a deaconess is parallel, or in some cases identical. It is disillusioning to those who have been admitted to the order of deacons to find that they have almost no time for these functions because, as one newly-ordained deaconess discovered, she had to spend the first month of her parochial ministry sticking down envelopes in a parish office; or if, as a certain deacon in the north found, he was not given the names of any sick people to visit, and, in fact, outside church he never saw or was spoken to by his employer. The Church of England maintains that it has the order of deacons. Angry protests are made by the Anglo-Catholics when any confusion is suggested between deacons, who belong to this order, and deaconesses, who do not. But in effect deacons are, like Samuel Johnson's definition of a lexicographer, 'harmless drudges' in most of the parochial positions to which they have been called. They are not given opportunities for mission. Nor in all cases are they given very generous help in developing their ministry or learning about its life. In many parishes they are just poorly paid secretaries, dog's-bodies, messengers and boilers of tea. They take matins and evensong (where those offices are still extant) when the vicar is away. The vicar wishes they would hurry up and get ordained as priests so that they can celebrate at the altar and thus be left in charge of the parish for longer stretches at a time. Deaconesses, who hold out no such promise of future usefulness, are even less highly regarded. A good measure of the humbug which exists in most diocesan bishops would be this: a woman going to him and saying that she wanted to be ordained priest would be told that she must be content with the job of being a deaconess and that this was a full and worthy vocation in itself. A young man going to a bishop and saying that he wanted to be made a deacon and not to proceed to the order of priests would be unlikely to pass a selection conference.

All but a handful (and that handful for the most part psychologically unstable) proceed from the order of deacons to that of priests after a year. And yet, as defined in

the ordinal, there is obviously great Christian beauty about
the order of deacons. A life lived as a deacon would be a
very good life, and a church with many deacons would
surely be a richer church. The scramble towards the priesthood which is encouraged by the present system perhaps
suggests a false theology of priesthood.

* * *

After the diaconate, the priesthood. After two or three
years as a curate, most priests will think that they should be
looking round for a parish of their own. This mentality was
not always encouraged or thought estimable. Arthur Henry
Stanton, for instance, became a curate at St Alban's, Holborn, in 1862 on a stipend of five shillings per annum. He
died as a curate there in 1913, having given his whole life to
God's service in that parish, to its poor, its outcasts and its
sinners. If Stanton is recognised as something of a saint, he
is by no means a unique figure in Anglican history. But
since the aspirant clergy, from their first ACCM conference,
are now treated like budding army officers or Civil Servants, it is not surprising that they should think of their job
in quite secular terms. 'Career clergy' used to be a despised
breed in the Church. It is now very hard not to be, in some
sense, a career clergyman.

It was more or less unheard of, for instance, until twenty
or thirty years ago, for the parochial clergy to *apply* for jobs.
Now it is common for livings to be advertised in the
columns of the *Church Times* as if they were jobs in middle
management. Anyone who 'applies' for such a job must
have a peculiar twist given to his sense of divine calling. It is
now perhaps seven years since he first attended his selection conference and was sent off to a theological college. His
response to the divine calling has led him through some
strange byways. He has put up with the stultifying atmosphere of theological college life. ('Years that the locusts
have eaten', as one priest described them to me; 'the
unhappiest years of my life', another. And another, 'a

complete waste of time'.) He has survived one curacy, and perhaps a second. Now, having responded to the call, he has got what he wanted, or what he believed was wanted of him. He is the incumbent of a living.

In a diocese where funds are tight (where are funds anything else?) the archdeacon will almost certainly think to save money by having an interregnum between incumbents. By the time our young clergyman is offered a parish, it might well have been vacant for a number of months. There are two advantages of this from the point of view of the diocese. One is that they are saving a few months of clergy stipend. The other is that when the living becomes vacant it is sequestrated and becomes the joint property of the archdeacon and the churchwardens. This enables them to suspend the 'parson's freehold'.

The inferior clergy of the Church of England are divided over almost all issues of doctrine, liturgical practice and ecclesiastical polity. It would be hard to find two Anglican parsons whose views on, say the articles of religion, disestablishment, when to take the ablutions at the Eucharistic altar, whether it was lawful to pray for the dead, whether politics should be mentioned in the pulpit, or any other issue, were coincident. But they almost all agree on one subject: parson's freehold. This is the sacred doctrine that a parson, once appointed to his living, can never be got out of it, except in cases of gross misconduct, cases which would probably require him to be tried in the Consistory Courts. Once appointed to his living, the parson is entitled to stay there for life. He is entitled to farm or enjoy the income of any glebe land attaching to his church and he is entitled to go on living in the parsonage.

Of course, in modern terms, this system is a diocesan administrator's nightmare. One of the triumphs of the campaign to make the clergy think of themselves as Civil Servants or middle-management men is to place into their heads the concept of a retirement age, a notion which would have been completely alien a generation or two ago.

Legally, however, if a man has been given tenure of a living he can stay there for as long as he likes. Some bishops blatantly *ask* their clergy to retire at 65, so that they can draw their income from clergy retirement pension rather than diocesan funds. Most clergy, by that age, strange as it may be to say so, dislike the idea of being in poor odour with the bishop and go easily. Perhaps they are anyway looking forward to 'retirement', that artificial phase of life which modern fashion has imposed upon everyone. (Father Stanton *retired*? General Booth of the Salvation Army *retired*? Pope John XXIII *retired*? Saint John the Divine on Patmos *retired*?) However, there are always the sticky customers, and to guard against having too many of them in the future many diocesan bishops, together with their archdeacons and financial advisers, suspend livings and only appoint new clergy to them on a temporary basis. They are no longer known as vicars or rectors, but as 'priests in charge'. This means that if after a stated period (usually five years) the diocese thinks to save a bit more money it can get rid of this parson and even, without too much trouble, wind up the parish altogether.

Nevertheless, in spite of the rampant warfare waged by diocesan administrators and by synodical wiseacres against freehold, there are still men being appointed to livings for, as their name implies, life.

'This is what I got ordained for,' said one parish clergyman to me, holding up a front-door key. 'A place of my own, a place in society, a *place!*'

It was not so long since he had made his ordination vows and heard the words of the bishop:

> In the name of our Lord we bid you remember the greatness of the trust now to be committed to your charge, about which you have been taught in your preparation for this ministry. You are to be messengers, watchmen and stewards of the Lord; you are to teach and to admonish, to feed and to provide for the Lord's family, to search for his children in the wilderness of

this world's temptations, and to guide them through its
confusions, so that they may be saved through Christ for
ever . . .

It is easy enough to sneer at the clergy and a good deal less
easy to say how on earth, and in their own parsonages and
parishes, are they ever to obey the ordination charge. What
happens first of all, after they have been inducted to their
first living, the parishioners have all had their first glimpse
of the 'new vicar' at the bun-fight in the church hall, and the
local clergy have drifted back to their cars, exchanging acid
little comments about the looks of the new man, is that he
shuts his front door and finds himself in a place of his own.

However fervent his hunger for souls, the English priest
is limited, in a particular time and place; he is limited in his
huge task, by the social history of the clergy, by the expectations which society, as opposed to his bishop, have
placed upon him or failed to place upon him. Perhaps there
was never a time when a high proportion of Englishmen
and women wanted to be taught, admonished, fed or
provided for by their parson. Certainly few would conceive
of his role in these terms today. If you asked the majority of
people, 'what is the vicar's job?' they would not reply that
his job was to look after *them*. They would probably say that
his job was to 'take services', perhaps to visit old ladies and
to keep an eye on any church schools in his parish.

The inextricable comedy of a clergyman's traditional role
in society makes it particularly hard for the laity to think of
him as a 'messenger of the Lord'. Such visitants surely
belong to the Salvation Army or the Jehovah's Witnesses or
perhaps to the entourage of Dr Billy Graham. The parson
who conceives it his apostolic duty to tell his parishioners
the Good News with the simplicity of these other organisations is a rarity. Nor is it necessarily the best thing for him
to do. In large urban parishes, where only a small percentage attend the parish church, how can the vicar possibly
afford the time to visit each household in turn? In the old

days when there were fewer people and a greater number of curates such schemes of visiting were practicable. Now they are not. Few men have the necessary skills for soapbox oratory, for missions on street corners, or other forms of outdoor evangelism, though in most large English towns there is usually at least one church which attempts such things. We have seen in our own time the development of Christian 'street theatre' and lay evangelism. But is a parson thought to fail in his ministry if he fails to undertake such activities?

While answering 'no', one is bound to observe the prevalence of clerical idleness in the Church of England. The men who sustain a sense of missionary zeal throughout their ministry (if they even had it to start with) are in a conspicuously small minority. Most men who arrive in a parish are concerned primarily with not losing their existent congregation. This is done easily enough, since in the Church of England many people see nothing bizarre about attending divine service when it is conducted by one clergyman, but staying away if it is conducted by another. Whereas a Roman Catholic priest coming to a new parish might be faced with the generalised problem of the laity not coming to Mass as often as they used to do, an Anglican priest is afraid that they will stop coming to church because it is *him*; or that they will transfer their allegiance to some other parish where the types of service or the appearance of the incumbent are more congenial.

The new priest in an Anglican parish therefore devotes himself to befriending the existing congregation, to soothing the organist, and to visiting those members of the congregation who are now too infirm to attend church. He would almost certainly love to change the order of service that the congregation has just got used to. If he is bold, he will announce his intention to do so at the first meeting of the parochial church council. If he is more timid he will introduce a lot of little changes over a longer period. Those who hated the previous incumbent will probably give him their keen support for a while. Those who don't like the look of the new man will decide to canonise his predecessor, so there will be an 'opposition' to the vicar within six months of his arriving in the parish.

All this takes up time and energy and, unless he is good at conserving and organising both, the new vicar will not have many afternoons or evenings left for his schemes of visiting, or providing more impetus to the youth club, or expanding the old folk's weekly tea-party into an opportunity for mission. Perhaps he has the prison to visit also, not to mention a number of hospitals in which he is expected to 'put in an appearance'.

When the laity speak of clerical idleness they are not always thinking of those rather amiable old-fashioned parsons who sat in their rectories doing nothing in particular. They are often thinking of the new breed of man who fills his day with bustle and meetings and paperwork, but who really gets very little *done* in the way of remembering 'the greatness of the trust . . . committed to your charge'. The type is familiar. He is addicted to copying-machines, stencils and typewriters. It is impossible to attend the simplest liturgical function in his church without having a sheaf of such papers thrust into one's hand. Side by side with complicated explanations of the diocesan synod, or potted analyses of how the vicar would solve the unemployment problem, there are whimsical requests for jumble, baking or garments, whose invariable exclamation marks provide such an air of frenzy. ('CALLING ALL KNITTERS!!' I read on one such piece of paper lately.)

This analysis of a parish clergyman's activities is not intended as satirical. Of course, in the midst of it all, we believe as Christians that the Lord's work is being done. Candidates for baptism and confirmation are coming forward, in little trickles, to be instructed; couples are preparing for Christian marriage; penitents are being absolved from their sins; and the faithful, Sunday by Sunday, are fed with the bread of life from the altar of God. So long as these things are happening, we cannot dismiss the 'vicar's job' as a waste of time. But the scope, extent and size of the expectations we place on a man at the time of his ordination to the priesthood are so great that he will never quite fulfil them. And the temptation in a priest's life must always be to accept his limitations and to lower his horizons. How many priests who have been vicars of a parish for five or ten years still feel the same ardour, or awe, or mystery, or whatever it was which first impelled them, years before, to seek ordination in the first place? How many have come to feel that if they keep the church fabric in good condition and their own existent congregation visited, instructed, preached at, married and buried they will have fulfilled their task? And knowing the ghastly embarrassment caused to most English people by anything which smacks of religious enthusiasm, or fervour, or a fluorescent notice-board, or personal expressions of piety, is it any wonder that most priests have shied away from the charge to 'search for (God's) children in the wilderness of this world's temptations'?

For, as well as being a priest in the church of God, he is also a vicar in the Church of England with all the semi-comic implications of the phrase. In England it is very largely a joke profession, a fact kept alive by such things as the popularity of Trollope and Barbara Pym, and by the conventions of television comedians who almost always continue to speak of vicarages as places where cucumber sandwiches are consumed by formidable ladies in hats, and where the parson's fatuous innocence allows a continuous stream of double-entendre to fly from his unsuspecting lips. ('I'm sorry to see that in spite of all my efforts there are so few young mothers here today.') There has never been a strong anti-clerical tradition in England in modern times. There doesn't need to be since the clergy have never imposed the least threat. They have always, moreover, come from predominantly middle-class homes and their vicarages, even if situated in less 'pleasant' parts of the country or even in the slums, have, at least in the case of the married clergy, brought 'middle-class values' to these outposts. ('It is the parson's job to teach people religion and his wife's job to teach them manners,' said one vicar's wife, still extant, to me.)

During the 1960s, many influential figures in the Church of England were wont to wring their hands at this state of affairs, seeing the placing of a priest in a particular role in society as a grave handicap to mission. One began to hear, particularly in the diocese of Southwark, of schemes to ordain uneducated men, or plans to abandon the traditional structures of parochial ministry. Some of these ideas were doubtless empty-headed or 'trendy'. But they were addressing themselves to a real difficulty. In the days when society was more fixed, the parson and the parsonage occupied a recognisable role; and in the days before the welfare state, the personal charity exercised and organised from the parsonage meant it was actually possible for priests to 'feed and to provide for the Lord's family'. Even so, as any survey of nineteenth-century parish life shows, they were handicapped by the fact that they were 'gentlemen' and even saints with the near-Franciscan ardour of Charles Lowder or Arthur Stanton had to toil for years before they attracted large numbers to church. Nowadays one is not overwhelmed when surveying the rows of faces in chapel at a theological college by their gentility. The concept of the parson's being a gentleman has gone; but so has the concept of the lawyer's or the doctor's being a gentleman. The 'vicar' nevertheless enjoys a certain status and, since English society is always upwardly mobile, one of the curious features of 'throwing the church open' during the 1950s, 1960s and 1970s has been to create a new clerisy, a new parsonical middle-class. Vicars are no longer expected to speak with 'Oxbridge' accents; nor do we expect them to have nice, old inherited furniture in their houses (though some still do). But for many men who are called to the sacred ministry, the prospect of having their own front-door key, their own house and a 'position' in society is beguiling. Some admit as much. Others don't. And few clergymen recognise how almost universally ridiculous they seem to the eyes of the laity. So the prospect of becoming a 'vicar' (that is, having a career in the Church of England as opposed to merely being a priest in the Church of God) still, surprisingly enough, has its worldly lures and temptations.

Nor should we be surprised at this if, in a time of high unemployment and financial insecurity, we consider what a clergyman earns. They are a notoriously poor profession, but in fact, in real terms, they are considerably better off than most schoolteachers, librarians or social workers. If the diocesan minimum of £7,700 per annum seems ludicrously small when compared with the salaries of doctors, or politicians or journalists, one bears in mind that very little tax has to be paid out of such a sum. Tax free and rent free, the vicar is given a house, and assisted with its running costs. Most parishes 'help' the vicar to run his car, some actually pay for it. If the parish has a generous patron (such as Christ Church, Oxford, who are the patrons of about eighty livings) the perks extend well beyond this range. They pay for all their incumbents to have a new car every five years. Any children of the priest can be educated privately at the school of his choice. Assistance is given with periods of sabbatical leave or holidays. Even in parishes which are less fortunate, the clergy can be seen by the genuinely underprivileged among their parishioners to enjoy considerable security. The bachelor clergyman living in a house which would almost certainly be beyond the means of half his flock still seems able to leave his flock in the hands of a 'locum' for two or three weeks each year and to return to the parish bronzed with the sunshine of Athens or Capri. For a married man the pressures can be greater, and fewer resources are available. But it has to be said that if no one in the 1980s resembles Archdeacon Grantly, nor are there many Parson Quiverfuls in our midst either.

The very mention of Trollope, inevitable as it is in any remarks one makes about the English clergy, reminds us of the somehow troubling fact that priests are human beings. We are all fully cognisant of this, and yet for most English people, even for lay people who see a lot of the clergy, it is a hard fact to absorb. Just because a man has been made a priest does not guarantee that he will find it easier to pray, or easier to be holy, or even easier to believe. Nor does it guarantee that he will find it easier to exercise virtue. And yet all the signals suggest that we *do* expect higher standards from the clergy than from the laity in these areas. The doting 'church fowl' who thinks that everything 'Father' says and does is wonderful; the disillusioned sneering of parishioners who think the opposite; the excitement and shock of newspaper headlines when a clergyman is found guilty of some sexual peccadillo: all and each these phenomena and a hundred others suggest very firmly that the clergy are not really human beings at all, but part, perhaps, of some angelic order such as thrones, dominations or powers. Those who despise and those who venerate their priests betray the same misapprehension.

It is perfectly right that we should have the highest expectations of our clergy, and that we should expect them to be diligent in prayer and Bible study, assiduous in pastoral zeal, just as we are surely right to pray that God will 'endue them with innocency of life' as the Collect for Ember Days puts it in the old book. Moreover, in so far as the priest mediates between God and man, and we associate the priest with some of the most solemn moments of our devotional life, it is inevitable that we should be amused or irritated if this figure has 'an unfortunate manner'. At one moment he is the priest of God, without whom we could not receive the Body of Christ. But only seconds later his maddening voice and intonation remind us that he is also Mr Plunkett who will choose hymns we don't like.

These expectations, which even the intelligent members of his congregation have of the priest, isolate him and if he is married they isolate his family. At the same time, much more than anyone else in the parish, the priest is on display and his family life, too, is open to the scrutiny of his congregation.

> I hated the lack of privacy that went with being married to a priest. I found this particularly trying when I was pregnant. What was to me a personal and private affair became everyone's business. I was fussed over, asked questions I resented and given attentions I found embarrassing.[6]

That testimony, by one woman in a symposium of essays by clergy-wives entitled Married to the Church, is only one tiny example of the difficulties facing the families of the clergy. Nowadays, the role of the parson's wife is quite different from that of previous generations. It is usual for a clergyman's wife to go out to work. Often she has more professional qualifications and a higher salary than her husband. As is usual in marriages where both partners work, the husband has to devote his share of time to domestic work and the care of the children. The stereotype of the vicar's wife never existed in real life, but a stereotyped vision of the role she was meant to play did exist and it is hard for a woman married to a priest if his parishioners still expect her to run the Mothers' Union, organise flower rotas, teach in the Sunday School and act as an unpaid parish secretary, if she actually takes no interest in these activities.

> Reveal that you are married to a clergyman, when meeting strangers, and you would be surprised at the reaction. People, especially other women, can be astonishingly rude . . . Fortunately I have a very understanding husband who knows that I would shrivel up and become morose if I could not teach and play the piano . . .
> I am not asking the clergy-wives of the world to unite and rebel. They have minds of their own and should be allowed to use them without any emotional or social pressure. But I am

asking that people allow us to be ourselves and not expect us to be cardboard cut-outs of the standard model clergy-wife, which is so firmly implanted in most people's minds.[7]

This cri de cœur comes from the wife of the Archbishop of Canterbury no less, and reveals the tensions and problems which many other women, in different circumstances, must have felt. While the rest of us can work out these things in private, a clergyman and his wife are always on display, and this often makes the difficulties worse.

In our own time, unsurprisingly, we have witnessed a huge increase in the divorce rate. The traditional Christian ideals of marriage are no longer upheld in society at large, so there is no reason why people should feel held by the evangelical injunctions forbidding divorce any more than they would feel constrained by those forbidding fornication. Sexual mores are notoriously 'catching'. If everyone else is having a good time, why shouldn't we? No statistician could prove the case one way or another, but most men ordained or subsequently ordained to the ministry probably 'consummate' their unions with their wives before they are actually married. The incidence of clerical adultery is much higher than many people would suppose. And, of course, since priests, like their wives, are human, their marriages are subject to all the tensions that flesh is heir to: the periods of disillusionment, the quarrels and the sexual troubles which threaten many modern marriages. It is not surprising therefore that the clergy should also be affected by the modern habit of divorce. The percentage of clergy families broken up by divorce is still not very high, but it is rising, and of course the consequences of a clerical marriage breaking down are more calamitous and wide-reaching than those of a lay family. In the stages before the actual break-up the strains are likely to have been greater because of the fact that the clergy live their lives so much under the gaze of parishioners. Then again, to whom could they turn for help? If the wife is a Christian woman, she would perhaps normally turn to a priest. But if she was married to a priest, and *that* was the problem, it places her in a situation of peculiar pain and embarrassment. Many clergy-wives, even those accustomed to making their confessions privately to another priest, would feel cautious about admitting, in open conversation to one of their husband's colleagues, that all was not well with the marriage; and even if they did seek such counselling, it would not necessarily be effective. The clergy who accept the modern doctrine that marriages can 'die' and therefore be said to be at an end, will inevitably be tempted to end the misery and sever the connection. Divorce is a painful enough process for anyone, not least for the children and relations of those concerned. But there is more than emotional pain and embarrassment at stake when clergy divorce or separate. Almost certainly, if a man's marriage breaks up, he will feel that he has to leave the parish and with it his livelihood, his house and all his security. Even if he braves it out and continues to stay in the vicarage, his wife still has to be provided for, and while the clerical life abounds in perks and small pieces of security while it is pursued, there is no abundance of spare cash when it is discontinued. Clergymen and their wives both suffer acute financial hardship in these circumstances and in spite of the efforts of Mr Frank Field, MP, the Church of England has still not fully addressed itself to the distressing demands of women in this position. The spectacle of a broken clergy-marriage is particularly wretched. So much prurient interest from the parish, so much intolerable 'sympathy', so bitter a sense of failure, not only in domestic life but in the priest's whole way of life. For if a priest is, as some have said, a 'walking sacrament', his marriage surely ought to be a model, a picture of Christian marriage for his parishioners to follow. And when it ends the priest must feel that the effectiveness of his ministry has been shattered.

'Marriage may have its pains but celibacy can have no pleasure,' was Dr Johnson's verdict. When one surveys the clergy of the Church of England one doubts the authority of the utterance. There are quite a lot of happy celibates, or at least gay bachelors, about in the Church, and in large towns and cities where there are many of them they can congregate and provide companionship for each other. The days are vanished when large clergy-houses were full of unmarried curates. But most bachelor-clergy in London, Birmingham, Manchester, Portsmouth and such towns see each other regularly for restorative sessions of clerical gossip.

Inevitably, a number of the clergy in the Church (married as well as unmarried) are homosexuals. In some circles one could be forgiven for thinking (in central London, for example) that *all* the clergy were homosexuals and of a particular tinge. But this impression is probably false. The 'high camp', particularly of the Anglo-Catholics, should not always be mistaken for sexual licence, nor even for specifically or solely homosexual preference. The 'gay priest', however, is almost as much of a standard joke figure in our own day as the formidable bishop's wife was in the days of Trollope. It sometimes comes as a shock to the laity to discover that a man who is fervent in prayer, diligent in works of charity, tireless in visiting the sick and the old and the lonely, and thoroughly serious in his understanding of the Church and the priestly role, should also be a practising homosexual. Considerable amazement was felt, for instance, at the publication of *Some Day I'll Find You*, the memoirs of a Mirfield monk and former Dean of Trinity College, Cambridge, Harry Williams, in which he wrote frankly and unrepentantly about his homosexual adventures.

This problem is different in kind from the divorce question. Every Christian person would think it better if marriages could last for life and if a priest's marriage in particular could be a harmonious pattern of Christian marriage which the rest of us could follow. The collapse of such a marriage is therefore a tragedy universally deplored.

Clerical homosexuality on the other hand arouses very various responses. Some people would condemn it as unpardonably disgusting and say that anyone who behaves in this way should cease to be a priest. After all, St Paul condemned 'men with men working that which is unseemly' (Rom. 1: 27 AV). Others would take the line that 'you can't help the way you were born' and that if a priest is dutiful in other respects he should be forgiven the occasional lapse. But others again, a vociferous minority, see nothing wrong with the practice and believe that the clergy, like other homosexuals, should proudly confess that they are 'glad to be gay'. Perhaps the chief objection to this type of clergyman – the sort who openly hovers about in 'gay bars', or, alternatively, makes no secret of the fact that the 'lodger' at the vicarage is actually his lover – is the pastoral difficulties it places in his way. A priest must be all things to all men. Many of his parishioners, who would not wish to pry into the priest's private life, would scarcely feel able to approach him as a priest if he has made his church and congregation into a 'gay mafia'.

Everyone knows that such parishes and such clergymen exist. Everyone knows that the incidence of homosexuality among the clergy in England at the present time is high. Most of the clergy are perfectly happy about this and do not regard it as a problem and are blind to the extent to which the laity might find it off-putting. The public utterances by Anglican officialdom on the subject are always shrouded in hypocrisy and allow the discussion of such questions as to whether homosexuals should be ordained to the priesthood, as though many had not already been ordained, among them some of the best priests in the church.

* * *

The great majority of clergymen in the Church of England will never rise above the ranks of the inferior clergy. They will continue to be vicars of parishes until they retire. It was to this work that they were called, and it would probably be true to say of most of them that they would not wish it otherwise. In some moods, they might feel like a change of parish; indeed, in some circles it is thought positively desirable to chop and change in the course of a priestly life and never to know the joys and sorrows of following a human life *through*: baptising a baby, preparing him or her for confirmation, marrying her, baptising *her* children, and seeing members of her family into the grave. Whether or not they enjoy the privilege of this sort of pastoral stretch, or whether they move on every five or ten years, it is to parochial work that most priests feel called.

But there is another category of clergyman who is altogether different, and that is the career clergyman. It is usually possible to spot them very young. For instance, they are much more likely to attend a theological college in Oxford or Cambridge rather than one in the North. Equally, they are unlikely to go for the extremes. Cuddesdon, not St Stephen's House; Ridley Hall, not Oak Hill; Westcott House, not Chichester; Wycliffe Hall, not St John's, Nottingham. These theological colleges have a certain chic (by the depressing standards of such places); the principal, unless he is implicated in grave scandal, is almost certain to be promoted to higher things, and will remember you with affection when, perhaps, he becomes Bishop of Durham or even Archbishop of Canterbury.

The really pushy young ordinand will manage to get himself a 'nice' parish in which to serve his title: St Mary Abbots in Kensington, perhaps, or St Mary Redcliffe in Bristol. However, it will do him no harm at this stage, so long as he keeps his eye on the ball, if he gets a less nice parish, for if he can say that he has 'done time' in some dispiriting industrial parish in the North of England, say, it will not look bad in *Crockford's*, or the curriculum vitae compiled in whatever works of reference take the place of that venerable book. He must not stay in the parish too long after he has been priested, or that would look as though he

lacked initiative. But nor must he leave too soon, for that
would suggest absence of seriousness. At just the right
moment, he should move on. It would be ideal, as a sort of
second curacy, if he could become the chaplain to a bishop.
This used to be a very conventional rung up the ladder, but
the sad fact is that fewer and fewer bishops these days have
chaplains whom they could subsequently reward with
plum jobs. So it is safer now to try to get some sort of
academic or semi-academic job. It is better by far if you can
become the chaplain of some Oxford or Cambridge college
*before* going to work at a theological college. It gives you
*weight*. Then, if you are lucky, you will become a tutor or
even vice-principal of a theological college. It does not
matter if you cannot get employment at one of the better
ones, so long as you are in the running, sooner preferably
than later, for the principalship. Alternatively, if you are
really a scholar you can stay on at Oxford or Cambridge and
become the 'Dean' of your college. If you are hoping to
become a diocesan bishop, it helps if you are reasonably
good looking, married (with 'normal' children and a 'marvellous' wife) and socially respectable without being
embarrassingly posh. If your father were the Duke of
Devonshire you might have difficulty in becoming a
bishop. If your father were the headmaster of Rugby, or the
Archdeacon of Chichester, you would probably have a
stronger chance. There still exist 'clerical families' of the
kind depicted by Trollope, and many of them are favoured
by the archbishop's patronage secretary. By definition, this
figure (whoever it may be who holds the office at any one
time) is a limited human being who does not know everyone and who will tend to like people with whom he feels at
home. He is unlikely to meet many parish priests who are
so absorbed in their work that they do not fraternise with
'influential' people. He is much more likely to meet men
from the theological colleges, the universities, and those
who hover about the persons of diocesan bishops. In other
words, the 'bishop material' at any one time in England

consists of a small group of men never numbering, perhaps, much more than a hundred.

The pattern would be to try the man out as a suffragan bishop or possibly as an archdeacon. Archdeacons have considerable responsibility and the successful administration of a diocese depends upon them. In rarer cases possible bishops are made into deans for a few years; but, on the whole, deaneries are offered to a slightly different category of man: someone perhaps with the gifts of oratory, or a scholar, or a clergyman with particularly social or liturgical graces and accomplishments, not necessarily 'bishop material'. In all these deliberations, too, the 'marvellous' wives must be taken into account, for a bishop's wife is much on display in English society to this day. It is essential that she be personable but not flashy or tarty in appearance; that she should have social grace; and that she be reasonably tolerant of, if not positively interested in, religion.

If all goes well, and you are married to such a woman, and you do manage to get yourself made an archdeacon or a suffragan bishop reasonably young (say, by the time you are 45 or 50) you stand a good chance of being translated to a diocese and becoming the Bishop of Durham, or the Bishop of Sodor and Man. After a sufficient number of retirements and deaths of bishops senior to yourself you will take your place in the House of Lords. It is because they might end up as legislators that the Prime Minister retains, and feels the right to retain, the power to appoint bishops, and it is unusual (though not unheard of) for prime ministers to appoint bishops of a widely differing political complexion from themselves.

Since the dioceses do not yet elect bishops, there is no other way in which 'suitable' men might be chosen. If you have at an earlier stage of your history missed the boat and failed to follow the sort of career outlined above, you can only hope to draw the attention of the patronage secretaries (the Archbishop's and the Prime Minister's) by establishing a reputation as a preacher or by carefully-judged antics which in others would be condemned as exhibitionism. Speeches in the General Synod if you manage to get yourself elected to it; letters to the newspapers (better *The Times* than the *Church Times*) and, again, judicious marriages can all help pave an episcopal career. But, in spite of this, there are many bishops *manqués* and disappointed career clergy in the Church of England.

\* \* \*

In general, the bishops seem an unimpressive crowd, though perhaps no one nowadays would echo Milton's judgment of the bishops in *his* day:

> Most certain it is (as all our stories bear witness) that ever since their coming to the see of Canterbury for near twelve hundred years, to speak of them in general, they have been in England to our souls a sad and doleful succession of illiterate and blind guides: to our purses and goods a wasteful band of robbers, a perpetual havoc, and rapine: to our state a continual Hydra of mischief and molestation, the forge of discord and rebellion: this is the trophy of their antiquity, and boasted succession through so many ages.[8]

Every now and again, however, a good bishop has emerged; not merely a good man who, by some extraordinary chance, happened to be chosen as a bishop, but a good man who was also a good bishop. The memory of Edward King, the Victorian Bishop of Lincoln, still glows in the collective Anglican mind, and his sanctity, almost like that of some of the mediaeval saints, developed with his unfolding sense of the episcopal function and vocation. In our own day, many people outside the confines of the Church of England have been touched by the wisdom and holiness of Michael Ramsey who was always, like King, a man of prayer and a shepherd much more than an ecclesiastical bureaucrat or a proud prelate or simply a senior clergyman.

For in spite of the unworthiness of the episcopal ministers, they do mediate to the people of God a holy function, and they are the inheritors, through the laying on of apostolic hands, of the commissioning of Christ himself. Great personal holiness is not obviously discernible in many holders of the office, but this should not blind us from recognising that it is in itself a very holy office. It is in fact the very office by which grace is mediated to the Church and to the world. *No bishop, no king* was the irate cry of the Scottish monarch at the Hampton Court conference of 1611. But Christians know it to be true. No bishop, no king of glory. No bishop, no Eucharist.

Hensley Henson, one of the cleverest and most tangential minds ever to focus itself upon, and to accept, the Church of England, concluded in his book on the subject (written in 1939) that in historic terms the episcopate had been maintained at the time of the Reformation merely for reasons of convenience; and that it was a hundred years after the Laudian developments in the early seventeenth century and the Restoration of the bishops in 1660 and the Savoy conference of 1661 (which ejected the clergy not episcopally ordained) before bishops were seen as essential parts of the national church. Then, in Henson's obliquely but confidently Erastian vision, the stage was set for the protests of the non-jurors and the devotion of the Tractarians to the doctrine of apostolic succession. 'The Church of England had always been episcopal, it now became episcopalian, that is, what had been a matter of practical policy became the requirement of religious principle.'[9]

In the failure of Anglican schemes for reunion with the Methodists or of the 'Covenant for Unity' between the United Reformed and the national churches, it is this ambiguity which has always been crucial. Would any ministers in the newly-formed church have to be episcopally ordained? The sticking-point has usually been that, from the Anglican point of view, they should be. Although the history of the Church of England would make it appear that the episcopate was retained in the sixteenth century almost casually, almost by accident, subsequent generations have seen something providential rather than accidental in the survival. The bishop, who in the discussions with the Protestant sectaries might seem to be the greatest stumbling-block, has in fact been seen to be the figure around whom unity will be found. It is in so far as the Church of England has bishops that the churches of the East and the church of Rome are prepared to recognise that it is a church at all.

But it is in a practical as well as a doctrinal sense that the bishop must play a central role in the Church. At his consecration, the man called to this office is told, in the words of the ordinal in the Alternative Service Book:

> A bishop is called to lead in serving and caring for the people of God and to work with them in the oversight of the Church. As a chief pastor he shares with his fellow bishops a special responsibility to maintain and further the unity of the Church, to uphold its discipline and to guard its faith. He is to promote its mission throughout the world. It is his duty to watch over and pray for all those committed to his charge, and to teach and govern them after the example of the Apostles, speaking in the name of God and interpreting the gospel of Christ. He is to know his people and be known by them. He is to ordain and to send new ministers, guiding those who serve with him and enabling them to fulfil their ministry . . .

One need quote no more than this to reveal how miserably far short most diocesan bishops in the Church of England are bound to fall from the ideals set forth in the ordinal. This is not solely because unsuitable men are chosen for the office, though in many individual cases this is manifestly the case. The combination of blandness and pushiness which characterises most career clergymen is not a very obvious qualification for a role which involves the stern necessity of upholding faith and discipline, nor the Christ-like qualities needed 'to have a special care for the outcast and needy', which is not the same as striking political poses for the benefit of the newspapers. It is quite possible, if the Church of England had bishops of the calibre which its ordinal requires, that the country would be swept with a religious revival unparalleled in history. But these men are not forthcoming and perhaps they do not exist.

Certainly, the man who possessed these qualities would be hard pressed to exercise them if he accepted the conventional role of the diocesan bishop. Bishops are no longer particularly grand or particularly rich, as they were in the past, though a few might continue to live in their ancient palaces, and most are granted fairly decent motor cars (Audis for archdeacons and suffragans, Cavaliers for diocesans). The disparity is not so much between evangelical austerity and worldly grandeur; it is more between what the Church tells the newly-consecrated bishop is required of him, and what it then proceeds to demand. Most bishops now feel obliged to run a large diocesan office and to pursue a lifestyle which would be more in keeping with that of a leader of industry or a senior Civil Servant. Surrounded by the secretaries, duplicating machines, telephones and filing cabinets, without which it is believed the Church of God could not survive, the bishop is directly involved in a multiplicity of largely secular considerations. How is the diocese going to balance its books, when it has paid for the clergy and sent off its 'quota' to the General Synod? Should it not realise the capital value of some of its more ancient rectories and encourage incumbents to build bungalows on the last remaining scraps of glebe land? Is it really financially feasible to keep this or that church open? Should it not be declared redundant? There is a debate in the Lords on education, or defence, or public spending. The local newspaper wants to know if the bishop is attending. There are dozens of letters from clergymen wanting jobs in the diocese, or wanting to leave, or begging for curates, or seeking an interview about some difficult question of parish administration.

Somewhere amid all these demands on his time the diocesan bishop is expected to prepare more sermons than the average country clergyman who has the whole week to think about them. No wonder the bishop's chaplain wears a glazed expression during this induction service or that confirmation. He has already heard this particular sermon three times that month, and probably he wrote half of it himself. Afterwards, if he is an extrovert, the bishop will enjoy meeting the people for about two minutes each over the sausage rolls. Then into the Cavalier and on to the next engagement, with frantic visions of his overcrowded desk-diary shooting through his mind. Tomorrow he will be blessing the new extension to the bypass, preaching at a school and trying to read the huge batch of papers sent by the General Synod about the nuclear arms race. Why, oh why, has he granted another interview to the Vicar of *****? And why, when he spoke to the wretched man on the telephone, did he hint that he would 'see what he could do' about getting him moved to a parish which his wife would find more congenial?

So, like an MP in a purple shirt, or a lord mayor with fewer perks, we expect the diocesan bishop to behave. At what stage in his life can he have time 'to know his people and be known by them'? A few, astonishingly, manage this feat. But none of them can avoid the burden of administration which is the curse not only of the Church but of so many other areas of human activity.

There is only one way to cut the Gordian knot, and that is to split the dioceses into infinitely smaller units, and to multiply the number of bishops by perhaps as much as five. The solution, moreover, lies ready to hand if the Church, priests and people were bold enough to take it. Every diocese in England is broken up into the so-called rural deaneries, groups and chapters of parishes, presided over by one of the parish priests, who is usually elected by his fellow clergy to hold the office for a particular number of years. In remote rural areas, as in the isolation of inner cities, the parish clergy are often intensely lonely. The rural dean is the man who can keep them in touch with each other. He is not merely an administrative busybody. It is his job to make sure that his fellow clergy are strong in spiritual things. Many rural deans organise quiet days or study sessions for their fellows, and since the appointment is no great honour, there is no sense in the rural dean's being anything but one priest among equals when he does these things. We don't *call* rural deans anything different. They do not wear special clothes. But when they do their jobs effectively, they are crucially important figures in holding the church together. Many of the clergy may joke about the rural dean. They probably groan about having to attend chapter meetings or open the innumerable brown paper envelopes which rural deans are wont to send through the post. But the rural deanery is an obviously workable unit in the way that a diocese is not.

Now, many theologians and historians of the Church would say that a bishop, almost by definition, is a bishop of a particular area, and that there is a peculiar anomaly in the concept of the 'suffragan' bishop or 'assistant' bishop or 'area' bishop of no specific area. For a modern diocese to work effectively, it 'has to have' many of these assistants to help the diocesan do his work. But it would really be much more sensible to consecrate the rural deans as bishops. The bishops could then know the priests and people of an area quite intimately and there would be much more chance that the Church's mission could, in those circumstances, be effective. The bishop could then be a father in God to his people in some more than purely notional sense. Without diminishing the sanctity or centrality of the bishop's role in the scheme of our redemption, the Church would then be free to make less fuss of its bishops as individuals. If there were as many bishops as rural deans, it would be simply impossible, from a financial point of view, to provide them all with cars, secretaries, offices and the rest; and it would also be unnecessary to call upon them to perform pointless tasks which could be done just as well by the chairman of the local Women's Institute or the chairman of the planning committee of the county council. Such a scheme would also compel the Church to draw its spiritual shepherds from a wider circle than it does at present. Does being principal of a theological college (and before that chaplain of a college at Cambridge or lecturer in theology at some university) necessarily guarantee that you will have the right qualifications to lead the mission of the people of God 'in darkest England'? In some cases, such men might make admirable bishops. But do we really need theological college lecturers in such abundance? At the time of writing, the Bishops of Birmingham, Ely, Durham, Kensington, Coventry, Chelmsford, and Sheffield (to name but a handful who come to mind immediately) all have this quasi-academic (and to be honest, in the eyes of the world rather third-rate) background. The primates of both York and Canterbury went straight from being principals of theological colleges to being bishops. As for 'ordinary parish experience' – i.e. being simply vicars – how many bishops can look back on many years of that? Not (again, at the time of writing) Lincoln, not Liverpool, not Manchester, not Oxford. London, Exeter, and Sodor and Man seem to be glorious exceptions; and it has to be said that they are conspicuously good bishops, who know their sheep and are known by them. Nothing remote or ineffectual about them.

The Church does not have to choose shepherds who will speak well in the House of Lords or at Rotary Club lunches; it does not have to choose 'good administrators' (good administrators are usually bad at administration and no good at anything else); nor does it have to choose men whose wives are 'marvellous' in the eyes of gullible patronage secretaries. Rather, the Church could look about for men of prayer and men of spiritual authority. In the

Orthodox churches, only monks can become bishops. It is not a rule which the Church of England could adopt, for its monks are few. But there is an obvious principle governing the rule, which could be taken to heart. Monks are, or should be, men whose vocation gives them more time than is given to those 'in the world' for contemplation, for the wisdom which comes from prayer, for reading, for learning and for scholarship, for cultivating a healthy balance between manual work and intellectual activity, for giving counsel to the broken-hearted and guidance to the perplexed. These are the qualities which would also make good bishops. The kingdom of God will not be advanced by administrative skills, cars, synods or parliamentary chambers; nor would it be diminished by one iota if every filing-cabinet, office computer, dictaphone or duplicator were cast into the uttermost parts of the sea.

* * *

We began this section with a bishop and his priests renewing their vows, in the middle of London in the cathedral church of St Paul. And we wondered how a Victorian bishop, if he returned to view the scene, would have reacted. The question was not intended purely as a piece of comedy, for it serves to remind us how radically, how completely, the Anglican understanding of the priesthood and of the historic episcopate has changed in a hundred years.

That change, once more, is in the wind, is inevitable, for it has been the habit of the Western Church to change almost as rapidly as the society of which it is sometimes, to all appearances, little more than a decorative adjunct. I suppose that a more radical question than what Archbishop Tait would think of the modern bishop and his clergy in St Paul's would be: What would Saint Paul think? It is his direct responsibility that we as Gentiles have heard, and still would try to keep, the gospel of Christ. And that is a bigger fact than the probability that he would be shocked by the pagan exuberance of Sir Christopher Wren's architecture revamped by William Burges.

On one level it is foolish to judge our own Church by the standards of the apostolic age. The Church has developed; doctrine has developed. And it would be completely impossible, as well as undesirable, to go back to the customs of the first century. In any case I mean something more searching. If the gospel which Paul preached is fundamentally true, and if Jesus died and rose again for our salvation, how do the clergy of the Church of England assist in that saving work? How readily would the Apostle Paul recognise in the Christians of late twentieth-century England what he recognised in his converts at Philippi, 'your fellowship in the gospel from the first day until now' (Phil. 1:5 AV)?

The answer in the mid 1980s is very different from what it would have been in the mid 1960s. When in 1963 the then Bishop of Woolwich, John Robinson, published his notorious little paperback, *Honest to God*, there was a reaction in the Church at large which now seems almost as bizarre as some of the squalls which disturbed the surface of the Victorian scene. The book was scarcely original: Robinson used, really, an opportunity for thinking aloud about some of the German and American theologians he had been reading over the previous decade. He was suffering from lumbago at the time. It is not the considered summa of a theologue writing in a library. It is the rather dull reflections of an honest-hearted rather donnish clergyman lying in his sick-bed. In the book he admits that he has often gone through phases when it was more or less impossible to pray. Moreover, he is troubled, as a bishop, by the divorce which seems to exist between people in 'real life' and by the old forms of Christian theology. Doesn't a lot of the language of theology depend on a scientific picture of the universe which we know now to be untrue (e.g. heaven being above the sky)? Does not a lot of 'religious language' make it sound as though Jesus was not really a man, but a sort of God in disguise who paced the earth for thirty years or so and then whizzed up again above the skies? Is it any wonder that modern men and women are untouched by these stories? Is it not the task of theologians to make the true meaning of Christian theology accessible to secular hearers? And would not a thorough popularising of some of the modern theologians be a help here? What about Rudolph Bultmann, whose Christianity was really purely spiritual and who did not believe that we could really know anything about the historical Jesus at all? What about Bonhoeffer, who in his last years in prison came to such a passionate conviction that we should try to work out a 'religionless Christianity'?

It is hard to know how far the bishop was planning to write a tearaway bestseller when he penned *Honest to God*. Easily the most probable explanation is that which he gave himself: that he was planning nothing of the kind and that the success of his book took him by surprise. Obviously, he touched a chord. The Archbishop of Canterbury, Michael Ramsey, issued a condemnation of the little book and then, having read it, retracted. Many churchmen, seeing the newspaper headlines and the fuss which the book caused, felt that John Robinson was cashing in on a public apostasy. His reply was touchingly frank and in the last degree naive: 'What I have tried to say in a tentative and exploratory way, may seem radical, and doubtless to many heretical. The one thing of which I am fairly sure is that, in retrospect, it will be seen to have erred in not being nearly radical enough.'

The funny thing is that there were so many people in 1963 who really supposed that Christianity was on its last legs, and that the bishop's innocuous quotations from the German theologians would rock it finally to its foundations. For all his radical posturings, Robinson was in fact a rather orthodox Christian who was simply distressed by the unimaginative use of theology made by his own Church. St Mark, St Paul and St John, for instance, all manage to preach the gospel to their hearers without making the slightest allusion to where or how Jesus was born. But there are still plenty of people who seem to think that the whole truth of the matter hinges on his having been born in Bethlehem as a result of a particular biological phenomenon. St Mark manages to end his Gospel with an unexplained empty tomb and a group of aghast disciples. This does not stop large numbers of people thinking that the *only* way of being a Christian is to accept St Luke's picture of tangible resurrection appearances over a period of forty days followed by the Ascension from Galilee which, to modern eyes, seems as though the apostles were present at a variety of launch-pads. The fact that other writers in the New Testament can use different ways of expressing the truth that Jesus and the Father were one and that after his death and resurrection he returned to the Father, taking all humanity into the Godhead and securing our redemption, does not mean that we label St Paul or St John or the author of the Epistle to the Hebrews as heretics. But a theologian has only to say that he prefers one emphasis to another for a proportion of the human race to think he is an atheist.

What has happened, however, since the 1960s is something which Bishop Robinson predicted; but it has not happened in the way he predicted. He said that in retrospect his book, *Honest to God*, would be seen to have erred in not being nearly radical enough.

To an untutored way of looking at things, this seems as though the bishop was saying, 'You may think I don't believe much: but you wait! The next generation will believe even less!' I do not think that *is* what Robinson meant, but it is a prophecy which on that level of meaning has nonetheless been fulfilled. In 1980, *The Myth of God Incarnate* made it quite clear that a group of Anglican theologians, among them those with responsibility in theological colleges for instructing ordinands, had no belief at all in the divinity of Jesus Christ, no sense at all that he and the Father were one or that he had taught his followers this creed. One of the co-authors of the book, the Rev Don

Cupitt (Dean of Emmanuel College, Cambridge), has made it clear, furthermore, in his other publications, such as *Taking Leave of God*, that he does not really believe in God in the conventional sense at all. God for him is simply an *internalisation* of our deepest aspirations and longings and has no external reality at all. To talk therefore of Jesus being able to enter our lives and lead us back to God – to use, indeed, any of the conventional language of prayer or theology – is quite simply meaningless.

This is not the place to discuss whether any of these theologians is right or wrong in their analysis of the issues. But what is quite clear is that they have had almost no influence on the way ordinary Christian people think, pray or worship. Side by side with the increasing scepticism of a small band of trained theologians and textual scholars, there has been a marked increase in emotional and wholly irrational forms of Christianity in the last two decades. The sort of religion which, in the 1960s, would have been associated with a Billy Graham rally is now a common part of Anglican worship. And not only has there been a development of the Evangelical party in the Church, and even in some quarters a discovery of 'pentecostalism', speaking with tongues and the like, but also a general firing, even in the stiffer High Church tradition, of the Christian community with what in the eighteenth century would have been called enthusiasm. The manifestations of it are not simply to be found in the friendly gospel music, the shaking of hands during the new rites, the experiments with liturgical dance, the bandying about of words like fellowship and (where did it come from?) outreach. It is also to be found in the obvious revival of simple religious faith among 'ordinary' members of the Church of England. Churches which twenty years ago were empty are now filling up again, not with men and women who are attracted by the refreshing 'honesty' of the theologians, but with those who believe 'the old, old story' in all its simplicity.

There is, I believe, a division in Christendom taking place

at the moment which is quite as great as the old division which severed Protestants and Catholics. It is the division between those who are 'old believers' (whatever new rites or words they use to express their belief) and those who are professionally engaged in dismantling the old theology. Theologians (in the days when theology was queen of the sciences) used to be the holy men of the Church, the men who were the experts in prayer as well as in biblical exegesis or speculative theology. The Church of England is not without such figures today. Although it is embarrassing to name names, one can see clearly that men such as the Bishop of Salisbury, Canon Allchin and Prof MacQuarrie are in this tradition. But there is another tradition of purely 'academic' theologians who do not seem, by the old criterion, to be theologians at all. What is sinister about them is not that they are freethinkers: plenty of people are that. It is that their total divorce from the life of the Church encourages the growth of anti-intellectualism among the enthusiasts.

The present principal of Wycliffe Hall in Oxford is seeking ways in which he can devise a theological examination which is a substitute for the Oxford theology degree. And this is because he believes that in order to do well in the theology schools at Oxford today you have to subscribe to heresy and to scrutinise the New Testament in a way which makes belief impossible. It is surely a sad day for the Church of England, which used to pride itself on its intellectual liberty as well as its joy in the gospel freedom, if theological students do not dare to ask academic questions about him who claimed to be the truth, as well as the way and the life. And yet it is surely equally sad if the so-called 'academic' theologians are so divorced from true theology that they close their minds to the possibility of the sacred texts actually being true. Tolstoy spoke of Ruskin's genius being one which was able to 'think with the heart', a phrase borrowed from Orthodox spirituality. There is not enough 'heart' in the academics' 'mind'. But, much more serious, there is not enough 'mind' in the enthusiasm of the new believers.

When Prof David Jenkins of the University of Leeds was appointed to the ancient see of Durham in the spring of 1984, he was unguarded enough to appear on television and say, among other things, that he had extreme difficulty in believing in the Virgin birth and that he did not consider it a matter of importance whether or not there was an empty tomb in the garden of the resurrection. There was nothing new in what he said. There was something very different in the reaction he got from that received by *Honest to God*. Bishop Robinson shocked everyone because he expressed doubts they had, for many years, been feeling themselves. At last, as the homosexual phrase has it, they could 'come out of the closet'. They too could admit that they had never quite believed as much as they said or in the way that they said it. But in the last twenty years, although the academic theologians have continued down that path, 'the faithful' have not. In the two decades since the theologians, after tentative humming and hawing over the Virgin birth, have decided to reject it altogether, the number of pilgrims to the Shrine of Our Lady of Walsingham has increased annually. Now it is not unusual for anything between 6,000 and 10,000 people to file through the tiny Norfolk village and proclaim their belief in her virginity. Likewise, in the decades in which academic theologians think they have seen the last of 'incarnational' theology or a belief in the actual resurrection of Jesus Christ, there has been a marked increase in the number of Anglicans who have. Should not parish priests and bishops be more bold and imaginative in approaching men in their congregations and suggesting to them that they should train for ordination? And could not this training take place on the spot? St Paul tells us that the Church has a variety of gifts showered upon it by one spirit. In any one deanery some of the clergy would have the skill to help ordinands develop their powers of oratory; others would help them through the difficult business of getting used to hospital visiting or caring for the old or the insane; others again would help them learn about parish administration and organisation.

This is all very well, they would reply, but where do we find the time in our busy parish lives to train ordinands? The answer is that they should *make* the time. The trainees, after all, would be potentially useful helpers, and, if there were enough of them, they would in many areas of life be like unpaid curates. Of course, they need some training in the intellectual life, and of course they need to learn the disciplines of regular prayer. For their academic study it would be necessary to pursue a directed pattern of reading, perhaps in evening classes, or perhaps in a few months each year at a theological college. Equally, they should learn prayer. Some priests look back gratefully to their theological colleges as times when they learnt how to pray. Others have had less happy experiences. There are other places where ordinands could learn. Where better, for instance, than in religious houses? The contemplative orders in the Church of England, particularly those for women, have prospered and flourished in the last decade or so. Those places that felt numbers dwindling and where it looked as though the order would fizzle out now have waiting-lists of young women who wish to devote their life to contemplative prayer. Surely, without disturbing the essentially withdrawn and quiet life of such places, some use could be made of their collective and discovered wisdom?

We must not lose sight of the ideal parish in which a resident priest prays for and with his people. But, as is everywhere apparent, the decline in the number of vocations during the 1960s, the evaporation of funds, the rather savage amalgamation and destruction of parishes which have scarred the last decade, make the realisation of this ideal quite impossible. While retaining the ideal, we should surely be looking for more priests and for priests who would not necessarily be paid, or 'full-time'.

Most dioceses now provide training schemes for some such alternative and in the years 1971–81 there were over 620 men involved in such training schemes.[10] How different it would be if there had been 6,000, as there would be if men could be attracted to dedicate themselves to the sacred ministry without the present unnecessary palaver of ACCM; without the expense and tedium of staying for two or three years at a theological college; and without the (still to most of us) faint absurdity which attaches to 'being a vicar'. Of course, for its rich ore of comedy, and for its great qualities of intellectual and moral excellence, we should treasure the social history of the clergy as a distinct class in society. But this clerical caste has now all but disappeared. In an earlier generation, almost every other parish in England would have living in its draughty old rectory a Master of Arts who, if no scholar, was probably a man of reasonable intelligence and reading and who would pass for a gentleman. We cannot view their passing without regret, but they will never come again. Today such men are teachers, lecturers, lawyers, accountants, architects. The new clerisy is quite different. But it would be greatly enriched if it were to draw once again on some of the old stock in the various schemes of non-stipendiary and auxiliary priesthood. In country districts, particularly, it would be especially valuable. The young professional man who could not be lured in the present state of things into full-time training for the ministry, but who finds himself living in a village where the church is only one of five served by the same overworked professional clergyman, could surely get himself ordained and officiate at the altar of his own village church on a Sunday? This would cost the Church of England almost no money, but it would continue to provide the chief, the important thing, which is the continuing and sacramental presence of Christ in our midst. The social history of the clergy has made us suppose that the clergyman himself is an important or an interesting figure in our church. So he used to be. Many of the most learned, or the most comical, or the most eccentric, or the most awe-inspiring men in English history have been clergymen. But that is a sort of social and historical accident. And it is essential that, with the disappearance of the social group, the Church should not lose the important thing. Nowadays the clergy do not have a position in society. Clergymen are not today, as they once were, *interesting*. But that does not matter so long as they continue to mediate the priesthood of Jesus Christ to the world.

At any one time, the Church of England, like most organisations, seems more concerned with its own internal workings than with the function which it is presumably meant to fulfil. It resembles a man who has bought a motor-car for the purpose of seeing the countryside, but who has become so fascinated with his purchase that he spends Saturdays and Sundays tinkering with the engine rather than speeding over the Downs. So, at any rate, to those who are not Church hobbyists, do many current ecclesiastical debates appear: none more so than the faintly ludicrous question of whether women should be ordained to the priesthood. It would be very surprising, to judge from the way things are going, if the General Synod does not, at some stage, find itself steam-rollering this measure through and forcing it upon (I suspect) a largely indifferent faithful. There are those who imagine – and they are not all of the vociferous Anglo-Catholic minority – that this action, the ordination of women, would, if it came, invalidate the entire priesthood of the English Church. For to take something which is the common possession of Catholic Christendom, the priesthood, and bestow it upon those who are not allowed it by the Copts or the Greeks or the Romans or the Russians, is to proclaim to the world that the English Church does not in fact possess that priesthood. Whatever the force of this argument, it is hard to see why this measure should be the sticking-point rather than, let us say, the consecrations of Protestant bishops in the eighteenth century. For whatever an Anglo-Catholic may believe about those consecrations, no one taking part in them at the time would have believed that they were giving men the power to ordain sacrificing priests. The individually false ideas behind the consecration of Protestants in the eighteenth century do not, in the usual Anglo-Catholic position, invalidate the Catholic claims of the Church. Why then should the individually false ideas behind the ordination of women in the twentieth?

On the other side of the argument there are those who would like us to believe that women all over England are clamouring for the laying-on of episcopal hands; and that since there is no theological objection to this happening, it should proceed with expedition.

Many people surveying the position of the English clergy towards the close of the twentieth century would see this as the key issue on which all else hangs. To that degree it is important. To the extent that it could cause an irrecoverable schism in the national church, it is important. To the degree to which it will probably destroy for ever the chance of any recognition of the Church of England by the Orthodox and for fifty years any such recognition from Rome, it is also important. But to the extent that it affects life, I would venture to say that it was a vastly trivial issue.

The old-fashioned phrase used to speak of a good priest as a 'great lover of souls'. That is the important thing. It is important to know whether England will continue to slither into increasing secularism and abandonment of the Christian religion, or whether there will be a return. There are many signs of revival, not least among a faithful and varied clergy of many different shades of class, background and opinion. Will the Church, the laity, the synods, the multifarious and superfluous works of pseudo-efficiency with which the modern church is lumbered, will they continue to enable the priest to do his job? The priest's place in society has altered, just as the Church of England's vision of the priest has altered radically in the four hundred years of his history. But the priest's task has always been the same.

It has been his task to seek out Christ in the poor, the lonely, the outcasts; to visit Christ when sick or imprisoned; and to feed Christ when hungry and to clothe him when naked. It has been the priest's task to raise up the penitent sinner and to pronounce Christ's absolution of his sins; and this is a task which the modern Church is worse than foolish to neglect. It has been the priest's task to stand at God's board, and in the breaking of bread to feed God's people with the body of Christ. That has been the priest's task in previous generations. It will continue to be his task in the future.

## NOTES PART II

1  *Dr Lee of Lambeth*, Henry R. T. Brandreth (1951), p. 128.
2  ARCIC, *The Final Report* (1982), pp. 30–9.
3  *The Life and Letters of Father Andrew SDC*, p. 133.
4  ARCIC, *The Final Report*, p. 38.
5  Training of non-stipendiary ministers will be discussed in the section dealing with the non-stipendiary ministry.
6  *Married to the Church*, edited by Shelagh Brown (Triangle, 1983), p. 71.
7  Ibid, p. 2.
8  *The Complete Prose Works of John Milton*, (Yale), I, p. 603.
9  *The Church of England*, H. Hensley Henson, p. 123.
10  *Non-stipendiary Ministry in the Church of England*, Mark Hodge (1983), p. 45.

PART THREE

# THE PARISH AND ITS BUILDING

*by*

*Gavin Stamp*

That amongst the several kinds of Buildings by which Great Citys are Adorn'd; Churches, have in all Ages, and with all Religions been placed in the first Rank. No Expence has ever been thought too much for them; Their Magnificence has been esteem'd a pious expression of the People's great and profound Veneration towards their Deitys. And the contemplation of that Magnificence has at the same time augmented that Veneration.

Such were the preliminary thoughts of Sir John Vanbrugh in making proposals for the building of fifty new churches under the Act of 1711.

The Act was passed to remedy the shortage of Anglican places of worship in an expanding metropolis: a shortage, it was feared, that was obliging many of its citizens to attend conventicles. The Fifty New Churches Act was also intended to affirm the commitment of Queen Anne's Government to the Church of England and to proclaim its supremacy in visible form, by great monumental churches. Rather less than fifty churches were built, but those that were – like St George's, Hanover Square, St Mary-le-Strand and Christ Church, Spitalfields – continue to justify their builders' intentions. Almost all still stand; most are still places of worship. To most Londoners and to foreign visitors, there is no conflict between architectural magnificence and their function as working churches. Such buildings look like churches and they are what most people expect churches to look like.

To many modern clergymen, however, the traditional concept of ecclesiastical architecture which lay behind Vanbrugh's remarks is at best an irrelevance. A prominent site and auspicious monumental character are not seen as assets in the work of the Church of England; the existence of large church buildings is rather seen as a liability for they involve maintenance and repair costs which the parish does not consider should be its responsibility. Churchmen are heard to speak of 'ecclesiastical plant' and to evaluate the usefulness of buildings purely in terms of cost-effectiveness. The result of this attitude, apparently justified by declining congregations and an increasingly secular society, has been more and more redundant churches, many of which are demolished – to the bewilderment and distress of parishioners (whether church-going or not) who still regard church buildings as the visible and reassuring symbol of the place of religion in the world.

Traditionally, the parish church has been seen as the centre of English religious and social life, whether it be a Victorian building with its spire overshadowing row after row of city roof-tops, or a mediaeval church at the centre of an ancient village. These are images which recur in English literature and which, at least in the case of the village church, have contemporary relevance. The parish church is lovingly cared for by the villagers and is visited by the tourist and the church 'crawler'. The latter may well have been guided there by *Collins Guide to English Parish Churches*, edited by the late Sir John Betjeman, who wrote in his introduction that he was inspired by a hanging sign he found in Somerton Church in Somerset. It read, 'TO GOD'S GLORY & THE HONOUR OF THE CHURCH OF ENGLAND 1782'.

It is highly unlikely that such a sentiment would be proclaimed today, not least because there is disagreement about what best pertains to God's glory and because there is such confusion and division about the very nature of the Church of England. Betjeman's *Guide* was published in 1958. Today, in most respects, it is out of date. Of the first paragraph of his Introduction, only parts of the first sentence still seem to describe the current situation:

To atheists inadequately developed building sites; and often, alas, to Anglicans but visible symbols of disagreement with the incumbent. 'The man there is "too high", "too low", "too lazy", "too interfering".' Still they stand, the churches of England, their towers grey above billowy globes of elm trees, the red cross of St George flying over their battlements, the Duplex Envelope System employed for collections, schoolmistress at the organ, incumbent in the chancel, scattered worshippers in the nave, tortoise stove slowly consuming its ration as the familiar 17th-century phrases come echoing down arcades of ancient stone.

Since 1958, nearly two thousand of the 16,000 parish churches of England have been made redundant and a quarter of those demolished. If the church is still in use, it may no longer be a 'parish church' in the accepted sense, with its own vicar or rector looking after the souls of those living in a precisely defined geographical area. In the country, the church may well be one of half a dozen in a circuit looked after by a long-suffering clergyman whose Sunday is spent driving about to conduct services in each. The village will be lucky if a service is held every Sunday: it might be once a month. And the old rectory will long have been sold and is now a private house. In the country as in the city, the church may well be part of a 'team ministry' which, again, no longer concerns itself with the old parish.

What is almost certain is that the phrases echoing down the arcades will not be of the seventeenth century and their familiarity will depend on how far the congregation has taken to Series 3 or the Alternative Service Book or the 'Missa Normativa'. Nor will the church look the same as it did in 1958. There will be a new forward altar placed at the head of the nave, raised up on a platform which is covered in mustard-yellow or pale green fitted carpet. Stalls will have been removed to accommodate this, and more stalls may well have been removed to allow the construction of the 'coffee area' at the back of the church, which may or may not be divided from the body of the church by a wood and glass screen. The profound changes which have taken place within the Church of England in the last two decades are most evident, and audible, within the ordinary parish church.

The triumphalism and self-confidence expressed in the Fifty New Churches Act, or, for that matter, in the church-building enthusiasm of the Victorians, are entirely alien to the thinking of the modern clergyman. No longer can he enjoy the status of a representative of the Established Church as that establishment can only command the active loyalty of a minority of his parishioners. He operates no longer with confident optimism but within a context of defeatism. That defeatism has been implicit in the thinking of the Anglican Church ever since the Religious Census of 1851 revealed that only 21 per cent of the population attended an Anglican place of worship (and half the population no place of worship at all), even though, in retrospect, the Victorian Age can be seen as the last great age of faith.

Today, however, the Anglican vicar is not just competing with the Nonconformists and the Roman Catholics. He is working within a society in which religion seems only to have a peripheral role. The Church feels embattled and more and more like a sect, less and less like the legally established, official religion of the land. The consequence of this is the increasing acceptance by members both of the Church of England and of the political establishment of the desirability of disestablishment and the feeling that Anglicans are but one 'community' among many. Indeed, the Church of England has taken the word 'community' to heart; no longer is the parish church seen as the visible focus of a secular, administrative entity, but merely as the meeting place of a particular 'community', a body of regular worshippers all known to each other. This is an attitude which merely exacerbates the problems of the Church, for outsiders – non-church-going parish-ioners – feel all the more excluded now that what goes on inside the church building is no longer open and familiar.

There are, indeed, many who would like to see the extinction of the parish as such, the geographical unit containing a number of souls whose care is the responsibility of the vicar or rector. The establishment of team ministries and the uniting of parishes tends towards this end, an end which would confirm that the Church of England is no longer national, no longer established. The parish church as a building still proclaims that ancient role, so it is not surprising that those who wish the Church to abandon its parochial responsibilities also dislike the encumbrance of a traditional church building. Without a parish and a public church building, a clergyman merely becomes a minister to an introverted and exclusive flock, one religious community among many and one which has no reason to attract the attention of, or command the loyalty of, Englishmen.

The obsession with 'community' in the social sense manifests itself in several ways. The most obvious is in the language of the new liturgies. In a deliberate attempt to return to the consciousness of the Early Church, the Creed no longer begins 'I believe . . .' but 'We believe . . .' This is to be found in both the Alternative Service Book and in the English translation of the Roman Catholic 'Missa Normativa' which is used by most Anglo-Catholics. It is a translation justified by theology and history, but not by practice, for even in post-Vatican-II Rome it is still 'Credo . . .' and the most superficial knowledge of Anglicans suggests that each person believes something very different from his neighbour and chooses just which portions of Christian doctrine he is able to accept for himself. 'We believe . . .' is usually a lie. Indeed, it was once the very nature of the Church of England to contain within itself a wide range of interpretations, if not of beliefs.

Post-Vatican-II Rome is responsible for another manifestation of the communal, sectarian spirit. This is the 'Pax', or the 'Kiss of Peace', which is practised in an increasing number of churches. Instead of the Peace being expressed ritualistically by the clergy in front of the altar, it is now obligatory for members of the congregation to 'share with one another a sign of peace', that is, at least to shake hands with everyone within range. Many Anglicans indulge in this gesture with ruthless enthusiasm, even though few Englishmen normally shake hands as a conventional gesture of affection. Many Anglicans find all this acutely embarrassing; on the other hand, they are anxious not to appear stand-offish so they join in, but the Peace can, in fact, introduce tension and undermine that concentration on spiritual matters which it is surely the purpose of corporate worship to encourage in the individual.

However, the individual is now seen, not as a single soul seeking his own salvation, but as a member of the 'community', who is required to indulge in communal activities as well as in acts of worship. This explains the growing importance of taking refreshments – usually coffee – after the service, a rite which often requires the construction of a coffee area, with sinks and, inevitably, toilets, within the church – facilities without which many Anglican churches have managed to survive for centuries. It has often been said that, for Anglicans, church-going is a social activity. The emphasis on the rite of coffee stresses this truth more than ever before.

But although church-going may often be a social activity, it is likely that outsiders will feel most excluded because of their unfamiliarity with the modern form of service. It cannot, of course, be seriously maintained that all Englishmen were once fully conversant with the Book of Common Prayer, but there are a few passages in it which are so deeply embedded in our history and culture as to represent a tenuous connection with religion for many indifferent non-church-goers. One of these is the Lord's Prayer, but, in some of the new rites, even this has been rewritten in the cause of greater comprehensibility to modern man. In fact the reverse effect has been achieved, to judge by the experience of one clergyman in the East End of London. He was taking a particularly harrowing funeral, with many silent, distant mourners, using the new Funeral Service. There was no participation by the assembled company until they came to the familiar words: 'Our Father . . .' The mourners began to repeat the Lord's Prayer until, embarrassed and confused, they realised that the clergyman was using different, unfamiliar words. The mourners stopped, participation ended and greater distress and alienation was generated. That clergyman says that he will never use the new version of the Lord's Prayer again.

This is an extreme example, perhaps, but it is a consequence of the change and confusion which have been introduced into the language and liturgy of the Church of England over the last two decades. It is true that there was not absolute consistency in worship before the 1960s, for the Oxford Movement introduced a division which led to liturgical research and the adoption of elements from the Roman Missal in some Anglo-Catholic churches. Furthermore, the Prayer Book Revision of 1928 (which, though rejected by Parliament had a considerable influence) resulted in a departure from the tradition of 1662, but it remains generally true that, despite differences in emphasis, in the use of vestments and other aspects of liturgy, the language used in most Anglican churches in 1930 or even 1960 was the same. This is true no longer.

Today there is a bewildering number of different texts used in Anglican churches. Not only are there several versions of the Bible, such as the New English Bible of 1961 and the Good News Bible of 1976, there are the various 'experimental' services permitted by the Prayer Book (Alternative Services) Measure of 1965. Of these there were three – Series 1, Series 2, Series 3 – whose permitted use was extended beyond the initial years. Elements of these services have been incorporated into the Alternative Service Book, which now has official sanction as the approved alternative to the Book of Common Prayer. Of its own two alternatives, Rite B is the more traditional, being essentially Series 2, while Rite A is Series 3. Many churches, however, continue to use the experimental service books and Series 1 is retained by many more conservative congregations as a reform of the Prayer Book which still retains the structure and dignity of the old rite. The use of the Prayer Book itself is rare, and it is usually for Evensong or for an early morning service to satisfy traditionalist members of the parish. Many vicars make it clear that they only tolerate the Prayer Book grudgingly.

Anglo-Catholic churches will not use any of the approved Anglican rites at all, however. In the past they may have used English translations of the Latin Mass combined with words from the Prayer Book. Now most will use the 'Missa Normativa', the translation of the Roman rite resulting from the reforms inaugurated by the Second Vatican Council. This has, in fact, many similarities with the Alternative Service Book, such as the 'And also with you' instead of 'And with thy spirit', and it is debatable which rite employs the more ugly and artificial English. Because of this, a few Anglo-Catholic churches will use a rite published by the Church Literature Association or one of their own invention which combines elements from the Roman missal with parts of the Prayer Book or the Alternative Service Book. At the other end of the liturgical spectrum, Evangelical or 'Charismatic' congregations do not feel obliged to follow any regular structure or rite at all in their services. It is all very confusing.

The Church of England today, therefore, at parish level just as at Synodical or episcopal level, presents no unified, consistent face to an outside but not wholly indifferent secular world. And individual parishes are often difficult to describe and classify as the old labels no longer have quite the same meanings. 'High' and 'Low' or 'Catholic' and 'Evangelical' still represent real divisions while the old 'Broad' Church seems largely to have disappeared. But these old classifications are now overlaid by other distinctions, as between experimental and conservative, modern or traditional, charismatic or otherwise, while the whole character of a parish, its form of worship, its life and its building, more and more can be defined purely in geographical terms: inner city, suburban or rural.

I have attempted to convey the nature of the varied parish life of the modern Church of England by giving descriptions of services at particular churches. These, I hope, may approach in interest those written by Charles Booth in his volume on *Religious Influences* in his great study of *The Life and Labour of the People in London*, published between 1891 and 1903. The selection given here is, to a degree, necessarily arbitrary and it is also governed by my being a resident of central London. My choice of services was also arbitrary and unplanned: I might well have seen a parish at work on a special day or on a rather bad day with an unusually low congregation, although my experience is that incumbents always exaggerate the average numbers of communicants. The emphasis given to the architecture of churches also reflects my own particular interests, but it is an aspect of the life and success of the Church of England which is much more important than many clergymen suppose. Indeed, there are many parishes which, despite the indifference or positive hostility of their incumbents to architectural considerations, would not function as well, if at all, without the appeal and authority given them by a fine, well-sited building.

\* \* \*

It is one of the drawbacks of living in the country that the Anglican has little or no choice about the church he attends. If he dislikes the form of worship practised in the village, he must drive several miles to find another, possibly more congenial church. It is this simple fact which explains the intense passions which may be engendered by the modern ways of a new incumbent in a rural parish. In cities, however, the church-goer has a choice. If he finds the worship in the nearest church to be too 'low', it is easy to reach another. As a result, few urban churches are parish churches in the traditional sense, for the congregation is seldom drawn solely from the parish. This is particularly true of the famous churches in central London, whose congregations are almost all 'gathered' because of the reputation of the incumbent, because the music is good, because the worship is spectacularly 'high', or just old-fashioned, using the Book of Common Prayer, or because they are just famous, established churches. The same is true of churches in inner-city areas all over the country and it is a not unimportant function of the Church of England to cater for the transient, spiritually searching or diffident individual who is possibly repelled by the cosy familiarity of his own local parish church.

There are many roads to heaven. Some may seem less direct than others, but the Church of England fortunately caters for those drawn to worship by snobbery or by a desire for respectability, just as it still sometimes satisfies those to whom glimpses of heaven are induced by music or language. **The Chapel Royal** opposite St James's Palace clearly thrives on its special status and some members of the congregation are drawn there as much by the hope of seeing Royalty as by the words of 1662 and the choir of boys in beefeater livery. Otherwise known as the Queen's Chapel, or Marlborough House Chapel, the Chapel Royal is not a parish church, but the Sunday services are open to the general public. Designed by Inigo Jones and built in 1623–7, it is one of the first Classical buildings to be erected in England and its interior remains largely as it was in the seventeenth century. The Chapel was originally intended for Roman Catholic worship; today, however, its beauty is dedicated to the traditions of the Prayer Book. All is done with decorum and seemly pomp. Gold glitters on the communion table; the clergy and acolytes are dressed in surplices.

On June 17th, 1984, between eighty and ninety attended the 11.15 a.m. Sung Eucharist and listened to *Leighton in D*. The congregation was smartly dressed and prosperous. There were some of those stalwarts of all Anglican churches, old ladies, but in general the congregation was mixed in age and sex. Almost all took Communion. The sermon was delivered by Canon Gray, Chaplain to the Queen, and Rector of Liverpool. His theme was the wide-spread children's conception of God. But in so established and comfortable a place, he obviously felt obliged to be mildly challenging: 'Our God is the God of change, of evolution . . . Where you see change, there is God', an idea which merely seemed incongruous in so traditional and unaltered a setting.

**St Margaret's, Westminster**, the late mediaeval parish church next to Westminster Abbey, also caters for those loyal to traditional Anglicanism, but the congregation here is not so smart nor so socially homogeneous. On March 4th, 1984, over a hundred people attended the 11.00 a.m. Sung Eucharist and sermon. Some were tourists who had drifted in and stayed; most had evidently travelled far to hear the Prayer Book used with straightforward dignity and to listen to the music of Wood, Merbecke and Mozart. Some were shabbily dressed; there was nothing grand about the atmosphere. The sermon was given by the Dean of Westminster. Afterwards, all members of the congregation were invited to a party in the vestry. Although loyal to the Prayer Book, St Margaret's is surprisingly ecumenical: it is stated on the service sheet that 'Communicant members of all Christian churches are invited to share with us in the Holy Communion.'

Another bastion of tradition supported by the Prayer Book Society is **St Giles in the Fields**, the ancient parish church which was rebuilt by Flitcroft in 1731–3 and which was once in the centre of some of the most notorious slums in London. Today few live in the parish and the church is overshadowed by Centre Point. Yet nothing seems to have changed, principally because of the stalwart, uncompromising rector, the Rev Gordon Taylor, a former naval chaplain, who was responsible for the faithful restoration of the church in 1952–3 after war damage.

On April 15th, 1984, there was a congregation of about seventy at 11.00 a.m. for Morning Prayer and Holy Communion. This was most likely a larger congregation than usual, for the Bishop of London was present to celebrate the 250th anniversary of the consecration of the present building. All seemed authentically Georgian as the bishop, clergy and choir processed up the aisle in hoods, bands and gowns, followed by assorted beadles and vergers. What was also authentically Georgian was the determined Protestantism which precluded any mention of the fact that the occasion was also Palm Sunday. Enthusiasm is not encouraged. The bishop rose to the occasion in his sermon. This dealt with unfashionable sentiments: that church buildings, like St Giles', matter because they are, 'above all, a sign and a symbol of the truth which God has revealed'; that it is necessary to go to church to worship even with doubts, for to stay at home is to deny the obligations of humanity to God.

At the end of Morning Prayer the procession trooped out again, to be followed by half of the congregation. The remaining half stayed for Holy Communion, celebrated by the bishop, but the moving dignity of the Prayer Book words was somewhat undermined by an unseemly noise at the back of the church, which seemed to be made by two vergers having an argument. After this an eccentric bearded man suffered an uncontrollable fit of coughing and had to have a glass of water taken to him. Perhaps it was just like this in the eighteenth century, if we are to believe the Victorian strictures about Georgian laxity. But the eighteenth-century Church of England survived on tradition and continuity and those strengths have gone. The congregation at St Giles' varied in age from late middle-aged to old. These smartish but slightly eccentric men belonged to a generation to which the words of the Prayer Book are familiar, but there is no younger generation to secure the future – the Church of England has made sure of that. It will be interesting, and probably sad, to see what happens to St Giles' when its admirable rector retires.

Another aspect of the traditional, established Church of England is represented by **St Clement Danes**, the ancient church in the Strand, rebuilt by Wren in 1680–82 and given a steeple by Gibbs in 1719–20. Unlike so many of Wren's City churches, St Clement's was very well restored after being gutted in the war. Like most of the City churches, St Clement's has a special connection to justify its existence, for it is the central church of the Royal Air Force. In a century which has seen two world wars and countless slaughters, this church therefore represents an aspect of the Established Church which many people find repugnant: an apparent identification with militarism.

On November 11th, 1984, St Clement's was packed to the doors, for it was Remembrance Sunday, that one day in the year when the Church of England seems to be an extension of government and the military. Despite the efforts of Lutyens and others to make the Cenotaph a non-religious and non-denominational memorial, it was inevitable that, in what was then a largely Christian country, the Church of England should annex the ceremony in Whitehall and create Remembrance Sunday. This is unfortunate in that the original and true purpose both of the Cenotaph and of Armistice Day is misunderstood and the Church is therefore often seen to endorse the worst as well as the best aspects of nationalism and militarism.

Clearly Remembrance Sunday is important at St Clement Danes. The procession up the aisle, over a floor studded with badges of squadrons of the RAF, by old servicemen was to the sound of the Battle of Britain march on the organ as well as the national anthem. Uniformed servicemen, one with a sword (in the seventeenth century ceremonial swords were hung on ornamental sword rests), then marched up to lay the RAF standard on the altar, a symbolic gesture the meaning of which is all too clear. Then followed the Last Post and the two-minutes silence. The hymns were all good ones with rousing tunes: 'O God our help in Ages Past' and 'I vow to Thee my Country', but the unremitting patriotism was leavened by prayers asking for peace, security and reconciliation between nations, creeds and races.

Fortunately the sermon was the real and necessary anti-dote to the conventional and complacent tone of the ser-vice. This was given, not by an Anglican but by a member of the Church of Scotland, Geoffrey Corduroy, Chaplain to the RAF. The theme was reconciliation, which must begin in the heart. The sermon was wise and balanced, con-demning both those who thought the deaths of young men in war must be futile and those who think only of the nobility of sacrifice, glorying in it and forgetting what the sacrifice was for and so giving cause to those who condemn the Church for endorsing militarism. It was difficult to gauge the response of the congregation to this call for reconciliation both with God and with their fellow men. The church was full of well-dressed and largely elderly men and women, medal-bedecked, with youth represented by a troop of Scouts. They seemed to be there for a social and national ritual; out of the several hundred present, only eighteen went down to the crypt chapel immediately after-wards for Holy Communion (1662).

**St George's, Hanover Square**, is a West End church which is fashionable for weddings. Designed by John James, it

was one of the fifty new churches built under the 1711 Act
and it has survived largely unaltered. In its religion, St
George's has moved slowly with the times, but remains
conservative, as suits the respectable congregation. It is
best described as 'High and dry'. The clergy are vested, the
choir – of men and women – surpliced. The rite used is
Series 1, the least radical of the experimental services. On
Passion Sunday, April 8th, 1984, there was a congregation
of about sixty, largely middle-aged or old and running to
four fur coats. The music – Byrd and Lotti – was well
performed; the sermon by the rector sound and dry. There
was nothing vulgar about the service, nothing enthusiastic,
rather it was dignified and devout. It satisfies a loyal
congregation which would not be happy with casualness,
spontaneity or trendiness.

Like St George's, **St Martin-in-the-Fields** advertises its
services in *The Times* and *Daily Telegraph* on Saturdays, but
there is nothing complacent or inward-looking about the
church. There cannot be. Prominently sited in the corner of
Trafalgar Square, it has for long been open to all and is a
refuge for tramps and derelicts. The work of Canon Dick
Sheppard, rector from 1914 until 1927, has not been forgotten. The present rector and his two curates succeed in
running a variety of services for the public and hold musical
events in the church, while never forgetting what it is
ultimately there for. There is a soup kitchen in the crypt
and a 'Social Service Unit' while the nearby 'Centre' offers
'A friendly welcome to anyone from this country or overseas, aged 16–25' with 'Music–Bar–Food–Games–Art–
Showers' and 'Disco or Live Music'. On the other hand, the
church itself is used as it was designed to be used two and a
half centuries ago. St Martin-in-the-Fields seems to show
that Anglicanism can embrace wider social responsibilities
without internal compromise.

The church, designed by James Gibbs and built in 1721–6,
was imitated throughout the English-speaking world and is

perhaps the most famous and most visited parish church in London. The interior retains galleries and box-pews. On Advent Sunday, November 27th, 1983, there was a congregation of about 150 present for the Morning Service at 11.30 a.m. The service was Morning Prayer from the Alternative Service Book, with occasional interpolations from the officiating curate, the Rev Charles Hedley (the rector, vicar Austen Williams, had conducted Family Communion at 9.45 a.m.). The hymns were familiar and rousing, while flute and organ music from the West gallery enhanced the traditional Anglican atmosphere. Despite the words of the Alternative Service Book, the worship was dignified owing to the structure of Morning Prayer and the absence of any histrionics or innovation. The sermon, on the paradox of God being a God of love and of judgment, was thoughtful and well delivered. All that was unusual was the congregation. There were many tourists and also many tramps asleep in the box-pews. The gathered English element was hard to categorise, being largely middle-aged and shabbily respectable, but the calm of the service was undermined by the tension created by the tramps, constantly arriving and leaving. One felt that there might be trouble at any moment, but there was none. A flamboyantly savage punk came in and sat quietly for about a quarter of an hour before leaving.

A very different approach to Christian worship is provided in another famous and old-established London church, **St James's, Piccadilly**, which was designed by Wren and consecrated in 1684. After severe damage in the Blitz, the interior was carefully reconstructed by Sir Albert Richardson. Today, however, St James's represents a powerful strain of modern Anglicanism which is concerned with social activity, political comment and various forms of 'outreach'. All this is owing to the flamboyant rector, Donald Reeves, who was appointed in 1980 and soon achieved sufficient fame to be the subject of an article in

*Harpers & Queen* magazine. Since 1980 Donald Reeves has established the 'St James's Community' –

> a group of men and women who are committed to a shared interest and concern . . . 'parish' has an imperial ring which is unrealistic in a secular, multi-racial and multi-faith society. On the other hand, there is a place for neighbourhood ministry . . .

– and the 'Dunamis Project' – 'a church-based educational foundation . . . to explore issues of personal, national and international security in the modern age.'

St James's has become a centre of activity, as the notices on the Piccadilly railings indicate. There is a busy programme of lectures and seminars. In a typical week in November 1983, there were lectures on 'Is God Playing Dice with Jobs' (by the Bishop of Manchester), 'Transformation of Unemployment', 'Psychology and Prayer', 'British Foreign Policy in the 21st Century', a recital of 'War and Anti-War Poems' and a whole day devoted to the Sufi Healing Order and 'The Quest for Wholeness in Our Time'. There was also an exhibition of Japanese art. Mr Reeves is also anxious to make St James's a home for artists, as 'our concern is to provide a platform for the struggling and unknown artist, and particularly to be a place where multi-cultural activities can take place (as a way of celebrating the possibility of a multi-racial society).'

There is clearly a contradiction between the remorselessly anti-establishment and radical tone of life at St James's, Piccadilly – Mr Reeves was quick to defend the right of the Bishop of Durham to 'speak out' – and the fact that these activities benefit from the church's being well sited, famous and an established Anglican place of worship. This contradiction was evident also in the pattern of worship at St James's. At the 11.00 a.m. Sung Eucharist on November 6th, 1983, there was a congregation of about a hundred. The liturgy was Rite A of the Alternative Service Book. There were three female servers in white, who did little, and a deaconess. There was also a retired bishop lurking in the sanctuary, but there was no important role for anyone other than the fully vested rector. His considerable histrionic talents soon emerged as he conducted the proceedings with easy familiarity. The anti-establishment tone was also soon struck. The rector apologised for the uncomfortable pews and looked forward to more comfortable cosy seats being installed – even though no Faculty (diocesan permission) had then (or since) been granted for the removal of Richardson's pews.

The sermon delivered by the rector took its theme from a reading from the Revelation of St John the Divine – a lesson appointed for the day in neither the Church of England nor that of Rome. The reading was one of doom and portent, being the breaking of the first six seals. This enabled the rector to talk about nuclear war and the evils of the modern world, but he was generous enough to admit that 'even those who want to install cruise missiles know that the world is a fragile place.' The sermon was an uncomfortable mixture of an attempt to be grandly prophetic and yet entertainingly chatty – full of asides like, 'Asleep yet?' and 'I said this would be long'. The rector would evidently like to perform on television; indeed, he revealed that he had been on TV AM that very morning. This enabled him to criticise the trivial preoccupations of the media, though he did not explain why he was drawn to exploit that medium. Most unconvincing, however, was the constant insistence that the Christian community was being beleaguered, like 'strangers in a foreign land', for St James's, Piccadilly, in the heart of the West End and benefiting from a stream of visitors, is scarcely like an early Christian community or, for that matter, like a modern church in the hostile urban wasteland of many provincial inner cities.

After the sermon came the high point of the service – the Peace. 'I don't want anyone to go away feeling that they have not been welcomed,' announced the rector. There was little danger of that: the kiss of Peace was exchanged remorselessly and with no quarter. Then, after the collection 'to keep the church open for all London and all the world for eight days a week, twenty-five hours a day', came the Communion. This part of the service was said perfunctorily, with less reverence than for the Peace. Also, contrary to Canon Law, the event was regarded as unrestrictedly ecumenical – 'All welcome to come up and receive the sacrament.'

But the formal, legally established forms of worship are of less importance at St James's, Piccadilly, than the desire for spontaneity and self-expression. Things only really got going at the end of the Communion when the rector invited members of the congregation to introduce themselves. A large number turned out to be American tourists; others were from Australia and Austria. 'I'm from Geneva, I'm a Protestant,' announced one bearded young man, who evidently enjoyed the service. Then the rector introduced that lurking bishop. It turned out to be Trevor Huddleston, former Bishop of Stepney and then of the Indian Ocean, who, now retired, was to live in the rectory. This was greeted by applause, Papal style.

But there was still more to come. 'Now would anyone else like to say anything?' Of course they would. Some told us how the Church of England had failed to come to terms with industrialisation; another described life in Southall. One lady felt moved to tell the congregation at great length about Hindu family ceremonies and what a 'lovely family spirit' there was among Indians. Finally, there was the Blessing, given in the name of 'God, our Father and Mother'. Then, after a rousing 'Thanks be to God', the rector cheerfully concluded with, 'That's it!' The service had lasted almost two hours; devotees then went to coffee and lunch.

A church like St James's, Piccadilly, clearly can do harm although it appeals to an odd collection of misfits and exhibitionists, but, fortunately, it is not typical of most parish churches even if the rector is regarded as a spokesperson for the modern Church. The style of St James's only works because it is in the centre of a capital city; Mr Reeves's activities are unlikely to work in ordinary parishes. And if the purpose of change and liturgical reform and new forms of worship is to fill churches, then the most useful lessons are provided by those parishes with an Evangelical tradition and an emphasis on 'Charismatic' worship.

**All Souls, Langham Place**, the church built by Nash at the top of Regent Street in 1822–4, has long been the leading Evangelical church in central London. Today its appearance reflects the success it is currently enjoying under the rectorship of the Rev Richard Bewes, for the correctness of Goodhart-Rendel's post-war restoration is undermined by wall-to-wall carpeting and by the rearrangement of the East end, with an extraordinary space-age pulpit console, equipped with a multitude of switches and placed on a raised platform. The lobby of the church is full of bookstalls, and the visitor is bombarded with literature. On October 23rd, 1983, this included an appeal for £10,000 to replace the church amplification system and a similar sum for 'Releasing the Ministry of the Staff (Purchase of Computer)' for, 'after detailed committee work and careful investigation, coupled with prayer, we have come to the conclusion that a good deal of our ministry is getting snarled up in paper and figures'. The parish is highly organised and much goes on at All Souls every day of the week with its various fellowship groups. The visitor is encouraged to become a member of All Souls – a membership not confined to Anglicans but open to all baptised Christians – and is given a membership application card which contains space for a photograph.

There can be no doubt of the success of these methods in attracting large congregations. At the 11.00 a.m. 'Guest Service' the church was packed not only to the doors but also in the galleries as well. The congregation was largely young with a high proportion of students and nurses. A choir of thirty-six stood in a semicircle behind the altar and there was a strong emphasisis on lusty singing. As well as the few formal responses in the worship, the hymns were all printed on the service sheet. This was necessary as even the most rousing and familiar hymns had slightly modernised words. The theme of the service was the 'Age of Anxiety', the relevance of Christianity in a world of crisis, tension and personal anxiety. The guest preacher, Michael Lawson, 'Director of Pastoring', did full justice to this theme. His sermon was in the best Evangelical tradition: long, intelligent, powerful and well delivered, with none of the mawkishness which characterised much else in the service. Unfortunately, its effect was somewhat diminished by a penultimate interlude during which the choir sang 'Forgotten for eternity', a modern hymn written by the celebrated Rector of Ealing, the Rev Michael Saward. At the end of the service, members of the congregation were encouraged to stay behind to talk to the preacher or other members of the All Souls staff about the message of the sermon. The notice sheet, which contained a blank page 'For Sermon Notes', also advertised tape cassettes of previous sermons available from the cassette desk downstairs in the hall vestibule. Also downstairs is the Waldegrave Hall, where the congregation was encouraged to have coffee afterwards, but its facilities could not possibly have coped with the several hundred people packed into the church.

**Holy Trinity, Brompton**, is another central London church with a strong Evangelical tradition. Serving Kensington and the West End, it is less conservative and more Charismatic than All Souls, but also manages to attract large congregations by the emphasis on biblical Christianity and on fellowship. Again, newcomers are invited to fill in a card and during the week many Bible study groups meet as well as other gatherings such as 'Smokers Anonymous'. On October 30th, 1983, the 11.00 a.m. morning service used the words of 1662 – the Communion Service once a month uses Series 3. The rather undistinguished early Gothic Revival building of 1826–9 behind the Brompton Oratory was packed to the doors, but in this case the galleries were being repaired and could not be used. The congregation was respectable and well dressed, of both sexes and all ages, but with many young professional couples. Many had arrived by car – the church could not function without its generous car park.

In many respects, Holy Trinity simply seems like a healthy, traditional Anglican church. Very different is the atmosphere and the type of worship at **St Mary's, Islington**, one of the most extreme examples of the modern Charismatic Evangelical approach. What goes on here in the old Georgian parish church of Islington, rebuilt internally by Seely & Paget after war damage, would seem at first to be utterly remote from the hard left-wing politics of the borough and from the trendy gentry who live in the surrounding terraced houses. But there is a connection in the deliberate informality and the remorseless demotic togetherness encouraged by the form of worship.

The 11 o'clock service on January 29th, 1984, was 'Family Worship' – Holy Communion is celebrated every other Sunday. There was a congregation of about two hundred, largely consisting of middle-class couples, many with children. There were a few blacks present, but they were outnumbered by white men with beards. In typical liberated middle-class fashion, the children were allowed to play noisily and obtrusively; one badly-behaved child running up and down the aisle was given toys by her mother out of a 'Harrods' plastic carrier bag. In view of the nature of the service, it may well all have been intended for children.

The service had no recognisable structure, nor did it employ any standard rite. Hymns were interspersed with a variety of informal acts or prayers or readings. The theme of the morning was 'Seeing Jesus show righteous anger' and, as it stated in the service sheet, understanding was assisted by members of the congregation: 'Steve and Sue help us to think about anger'. This they did with a series of mime acts, illustrating such events as railway passengers arguing about opening and shutting the window, while over the amplification system came a series of statistics about world poverty, nuclear weapons and other matters of concern. Steve and Sue both wore jeans and bright red T-shirts; Steve being distinguished from Sue by his large black beard. At the end of each mime act came the refrain, 'Is this what makes you angry?' a question which might well have provoked a different answer to that expected by the actors.

After more hymns and lessons, the rector appeared on stage. I assume he was the rector, the Rev Graham Claydon, because if he was wearing a clerical collar it was concealed by his remarkably colourful jumper. This gentleman led a chorus, with piano and tambourine accompaniment. The congregation were encouraged to wave their arms in the air during this, and they did. After inviting all the children to go out and join their various 'groups', he then introduced Joanne, who had been working for CSV in Islington with 'young people in an out-of-work situation'. Joanne then took the stage to tell us why she liked coming to St Mary's. It was because she had received a 'good welcome' there when she had first arrived. Having linked up with a 'home group', she had managed to make friends in the area.

Geoff and Elaine then led the prayers, and expressed the hope that we should not judge people by 'clothes and manners and other irrelevant things'. Suddenly one was reminded that this was the parish church of Islington. The sermon, however, returned to an older and more vital Evangelical tradition, for it was professional and not deliberately amateur and informal. It was also lucid, being delivered by the Rev Pete Broadbent, Chaplain to the

Polytechnic of North London, as well as a Labour councillor
in Islington, who felt able to wear clerical dress. The text
was John 2:16 (GNB), 'Stop making my Father's house a
market-place', and he dealt with how God is 'not concerned
to have his temple soiled by shoddy commercialism'.
St Mary's, Islington, is certainly not soiled by any such
thing; unfortunately, it does not seem like a temple at all.

The well-established Anglo-Catholic churches of central
London are also still able to draw large congregations, if not
so large as the Evangelical churches. They also, inevitably,
draw a different sort of congregation, attracted by music,
tradition and liturgy, although several also have an emphasis on belonging and on fellowship which they share
with the Evangelicals.

**All Saints', Margaret Street**, the famous church built by
A. J. Beresford-Hope in the 1850s and which was the first
polychromatic masterpiece of William Butterfield, has for
long been the leading Anglo-Catholic church in London.
Practically nothing has changed since the early years of this
century and the atmosphere inside remains dark, powerful
and numinous.

At the 11 o'clock High Mass and sermon on October 2nd,
1983, there was a congregation of over two hundred, mixed
in sex and age, largely well dressed and respectable, but
leavened by the more eccentric figures typical of Anglo-
Catholic churches. Priests and deacons were all fully
vested; there were eight servers in the sanctuary and there
was a choir of nine – including four women. The liturgy was
Series 1, done with dignity and precision. The sermon, by
the curate, Fr Young, was a little self-satisfied, being on the
theme of All Saints' being the house of God and 'A haven of
Peace', although presumably the congregation did not
need to be told that as it was why they were there. Afterwards sherry was served in the courtyard, where there
were stalls at which special All Saints' ties, key-rings and
T-shirts could be purchased. The atmosphere was that of a

jolly, intimate party. All Saints', Margaret Street, is still clearly a healthy metropolitan church, although it has contracted in recent years. The choir school has closed and many of the assets of the church were realised by the Rev Michael Marshall, before becoming Bishop of Woolwich, to establish the Christian Centre, a venture which has since flopped.

**St Mary's, Bourne Street**, near Sloane Square, has for long regarded itself as the most important Anglo-Catholic church in London. A red-brick mission church of the 1870s cleverly fitted out in the early twentieth century, thanks to Lord Halifax and other grand patrons, with a baroque high altar and other devotional fittings, St Mary's seems and is meant to seem like a Roman Catholic church. For the benefit of visitors, the vicar, the Rev John Gilling, has written a helpful explanatory leaflet for those who wonder, 'What kind of church is this?' Entitled, 'Why so High?' this recounts how Princess Alexandra, who admired the architecture and decoration of St Mary's, asked 'And is it the highest church in London?' Explaining the Catholic tradition of the church, the vicar concludes with the admirably Anglican and ecumenical sentiment that 'every Christian community, like each one of us, is individual and unique. Yet we are all members of the one Church of God founded by Jesus for the salvation of all men.'

At the High Mass at 11 o'clock on March 18th, 1984, there was a congregation of about eighty. In the sanctuary there were two priests and one deacon and six assorted servers and acolytes, all suitably vested. St Mary's retains the arcane and sophisticated character which has for long made it a special place for many who find no home in other congregations. The late Lord Bradwell (Tom Driberg) was married here, with some pomp. But now, having for long used their own rite, the clergy have introduced a new service book with alternatives derived from Rite A of the ASB: alternatives which may dispense with the language of the Prayer Book and the Roman missal which is evidently preferred by many of the regular congregation. And the congregation was well dressed and respectable, varying in age from old people to noisy children, who succeeded in negating the purpose of the well-sung Palestrina coming from the choir in the West gallery.

The sermon was delivered by the curate, Fr Bugby, who sported a luxuriant moustache, despite this form of facial hair being prohibited by Canon Law. The sermon was on the Thanksgiving, as part of a Lenten series on the Eucharist, and was arch and self-conscious. References to Dr Mascall, the distinguished theologian on the staff of St Mary's, merely increased the cosy and introverted, albeit also devout and spiritual, atmosphere of the place. St Mary's is very much a church catering for a gathered congregation, something only possible in the centre of a city. Its actual parish is very small indeed, much smaller than that of St Barnabas', Pimlico, just down the road, which is run by considerably fewer staff. But St Mary's is open every day and mass is said twice on some weekdays.

**St Alban's, Holborn**, one of the great Anglo-Catholic slum churches of the nineteenth century, seems rather less introverted, although the traditions set by Fr Mackonochie and Fr Stanton have not been forgotten. The original tough polychromatic Gothic building by Butterfield was gutted in the war and, as rebuilt by Giles and Adrian Gilbert Scott, has an interior which is tall, white and spacious and dominated by an extraordinary mural on the East wall by Hans Feibusch.

At the 11 o'clock Solemn Mass on January 15th, 1984, there was a congregation of about ninety. Although there were many of the sort of young men long associated with St Alban's there were also women and several children. Indeed, after the sermon there was a baptism, for which the highly professional choir had been augmented in number. The music was imaginative: Vaughan Williams and

Messaien. Two priests and the deacon were clad in modern vestments whose single merit was that they harmonised with the colours of the mural. There were also nine acolytes and servers and, perhaps surprisingly, a deaconess, dressed in white, who sat on one side of the sanctuary looking rather superfluous and a little sad. The liturgy itself – a version of the 'Missa Normativa' published by the Church Literature Association – was performed with particular dignity and with no affectation. Afterwards, in the dingy hall of the old St Alban's school (which it is hoped to replace by flats and a new church hall), sherry was served – post-liturgical alcohol rather than coffee being one principal distinction between Anglo-Catholic and Evangelical gatherings. St Alban's seemed a particularly healthy church, if with a gathered rather than a local congregation.

The Tractarians were active in building churches in the poorest parts of London, and today it is often only Anglo-Catholic churches which still survive in such places. In Shoreditch in the 1860s the Haggerston Church Scheme was responsible for building six new churches; today only two of them remain in use and both are 'high'. One is **St Anne's, Hoxton**, a ragstone Gothic building of little architectural distinction, whose parish is combined with those of two demolished churches. A few hundred yards away is St Columba's, once one of the famous Tractarian churches of East London and the masterpiece of James Brooks. This vast and impressive building has been closed and is now leased to a Nigerian sect. St Anne's has one of the toughest parishes in London, where black immigrants mix with an old-established Cockney population. The area is notorious for crime and for racial tension.

Although in the heart of a very deprived inner-urban area, St Anne's was for long threatened with closure. In 1965 the presentation of the living was suspended and the parish was linked for a time with that of Holy Trinity, Hoxton. In 1980 Anthony Symondson was appointed priest-in-charge, and it has been his achievement to secure the future of St Anne's. A permanent vicarage has been built in Hemsworth Street next to the church hall and, in 1985, the suspension was at last lifted by the Stepney area pastoral committee. Fr Symondson has also succeeded in greatly improving the interior. The church has been reordered with good quality furniture rescued from neighbouring redundant churches and made harmonious with sensitive colouring and marbling. The forward altar, a Neoclassical piece of 1900, must be one of the most handsome in the country and, as all the work cost less than £1,000, the interior contrasts most favourably with the standard, very expensive reorderings of churches which usually result in discordant new platforms and furniture with mustard-coloured or pale-green close carpeting and unstained wood. St Anne's, although perfectly adapted to the new liturgy, looks as if it has not been changed, which is as its incumbent intended.

At the Parish Mass at 11 o'clock on July 1st, 1984, a sunny summer morning, the church at first seemed empty, but the congregation drifted in eventually to make a total of thirty-four – two-thirds black and with many young girls. The liturgy was from the 'Missa Normativa' in the form of the Church Union's Eucharist No. 5 book. There were four in the sanctuary: three black servers and acolytes. No organ played as the organist was ill and not expected to return. The atmosphere was one of calm familiarity with the form of worship and the Peace was celebrated with conspicuous enthusiasm. In the sermon, Fr Symondson did not talk down to the congregation; his theme was the nature of the priesthood, emphasising that the priest was a servant of the parish and not an authoritarian figure. Simultaneous with the service was a Sunday School run by a nun from St Saviour's Priory. Of the eight children, only one, called Wesley, was white. St Anne's does much for local children: the following Saturday there was a trip to the country for them and at 5 o'clock every Sunday there is a Bible study class. Fr Symondson's chief complaint with the parish is that he cannot depend on initiative from the laity such as occurs in middle-class churches.

At the end of 1985 Anthony Symondson resigned as priest-in-charge of St Anne's and was received into the Roman Catholic Church. He did not take this decision lightly and found it painful to leave Hoxton, but he found that he could no longer cope with the apparently irreconcilable conflicts of churchmanship within the Church of England, and that Anglo-Catholic life in London had become intolerably desiccated.

The Church of the **Holy Cross, Cromer Street**, in King's Cross is another long-established Anglo-Catholic mission church, built in the 1880s in part of the old parish of St Pancras. The Gothic Revival brick building is now surrounded by council flats. Holy Cross had the doubtful distinction in 1982 of having been occupied for twelve days by women calling themselves the English Collective of Prostitutes in protest at the police action to clean up vice in the area.

At the Midnight Mass at 11.30 p.m. on Christmas Eve, 1983, there was a congregation of about sixty, half of whom were not regular attenders. There was the usual tension present in an urban parish on this occasion because of the risk that the proceedings might be disrupted by maudlin or difficult drunks from the nearby pub. In the event the congregation was scandalised by the giggling and necking of rather different intruders: four brightly coloured punks who claimed to be members of the Gay Christian Movement. After carols and readings by local children, the liturgy began, using the New Roman Rite (many strangers assume Holy Cross is a Roman Catholic church). With two priests, two servers and two acolytes, the liturgy was dignified despite confusion which made precision impossible. Although it was Christmas, the parish priest, Fr Trevor Richardson, gave a gloomy and belligerent sermon, commenting on local violence and on what Christianity could mean in the area when both the English language and the Christian religion were in a minority in the local primary school.

More typical of the Church of England in amorphous urban areas is a church like **St Gabriel's, Warwick Square**. Like other Pimlico churches, this is a dull ragstone Gothic church of the 1840s by Cundy but its steeple is an important landmark among the surrounding terraces. Unfortunately the building is falling down and may well not survive. St Gabriel's looks like a middle-class, middle-of-the-road church. The main service is at 10.30 a.m., preceded by Matins at 9.45 and a 'traditional language' Mass at 8.15. It has been made moderately 'high' by the present incumbent, Fr David Skeoch, the former Chaplain to the Bishop of London, so Evensong at 6.30 p.m. is now followed by Benediction.

St Gabriel's has a vicar and two curates. At the Sung Mass and sermon on September 9th, 1984, one curate was on holiday and Fr Skeoch was away preaching at his old haunt, St Mary's, Bourne Street (p. 161). The service was taken by the second curate, Fr Young who, like the deacon, sported an uncanonical moustache. There were four servers and acolytes and a choir of three robed girls and a surpliced man. The ASB Rite A was used and a forward nave altar rendered the chancel entirely redundant. The congregation numbered about thirty-five, of whom six were men and three children. Most seemed to be old and respectable denizens of Warwick Square, who were traditional Anglicans, yet St Gabriel's now has a vast parish which includes Churchill Gardens, the large post-war Pimlico housing estate built by the City of Westminster. With its two curates, St Gabriel's is regarded as a 'training parish', but, despite the two curates, little impact seems to have been made in the wider area. Whether the church will be more successful if it has to move to a church hall geographically more in the centre of the parish is open to question. The real question, however, is why St Gabriel's is so well endowed with staff by the diocese when the neighbouring parish of St Barnabas, Pimlico, which has always been working-class, has no curate (and was threatened with closure) and many East End parishes are similarly under-staffed.

**St Mary's, Stoke Newington**, has a curate, which it needs. The strength of the Church of England is often felt to be in the suburbs, but Stoke Newington is really neither urban nor suburban. It is a village swallowed up by North-East London in the mid-nineteenth century and now has a large black and Jewish population. Fortunately the presence of the Church is proclaimed by the new church of St Mary's, a large and fine example of the work of Sir Gilbert Scott, built in the 1850s, the spire of which is a prominent landmark for miles around. (The old church, over the road, a charming ramshackle building of many centuries, is now used by Nigerians of Christ's Apostolic Church.)

It is reassuring to find that the importance of the building is appreciated by the clergy, for, as the curate, Stephen Coles, wrote in the parish newsletter,

We at this church, named after Mary, are . . . not here just for ourselves. We worship on behalf of all and we have a special responsibility to enable Jesus to be born in Stoke Newington now. This has to happen in each generation everywhere in the world. That's one of the reasons why this country is divided into parishes, each with a church. The church is a constant reminder of the presence of God in a place. The building is a reminder of the believers, who worship there.

It is also an advantage sometimes to have a church of architectural distinction, for the vestry has been restored after an outbreak of dry rot with the help of grants totalling £70,000 from the Department of the Environment and the Greater London Council.

At the 10.30 a.m. parish Communion on December 18th, 1983, there was a congregation of about a hundred, largely filling the building. Many of these were children: the black ones quiet and well behaved, the white ones noisy and undisciplined. The curate thought numbers were down because the Christmas carol service was taking place that evening. Those present were mixed in age and sex, with perhaps one-fifth being black. The liturgy was the more conservative ASB Rite B but the church seemed full of life and the congregation united. That morning six people were commissioned to give the chalice at Communion. Refreshments were served afterwards in the basement of the adjacent rectory, and much goes on there during the week connected with the church: discussion and house groups, the youth club, Mothers' Union, the Scouts, etc., as well as daily services.

The parish of **St Mary's, Barnes**, is more wealthy and certainly more middle-class, and it has triumphantly survived a disaster which might have been catastrophic had the pessimism current in the Church of England been allowed to prevail. In 1978 the old parish church of Barnes, part mediaeval, part Victorian, was destroyed by an arsonist. It was decided to rebuild, but the manner of rebuilding caused much controversy, which divided the parish. Many living locally wanted the building restored as it was, but the parish church council eventually decided to commission a new design. The architect chosen, Edward Cullinan, had never built a church before but, owing in part to local criticism, the result cleverly incorporates parts of the old structure into a new building which has traditional overtones. At the same time the church has been reorientated North-South, creating a large centralised space for modern worship. The rebuilt church is something of a triumph; illustrated in all the architectural journals; it also satisfies the needs of the parish and is clearly, recognisably, a church. As the rector remarked, 'We've got a winner.'

At the 10.00 a.m. parish Communion on September 16th, 1984 – not long after the reopening of the church – there was a congregation of over eighty, varied in age and representative of the local population. The seating was grouped on three sides of a forward altar, behind which were seated two clergy, a deaconess and six others – whose function seemed uncertain – all in white albs. The liturgy used was the ASB Rite B, though the more traditional language of this was upset by readings from the New English Bible. During the Communion about twenty children from the 'junior church' came in and then went out into their own room. The sermon by the rector mentioned how 'much prayer went into the rebuilding of this church' and stressed how prayer was now needed to rebuild the parish spiritually. As the new St Mary's is a building Barnes will soon be proud of, this ought not to be too difficult and the positive attitude of the parish is in marked contrast to the apathy and betrayal so often produced by the Church of England's neglect and wilful abandonment of fine buildings. In the case of Barnes parish church, the insurance money from the fire was insufficient to erect the new building and the rest of the money was raised locally.

**Christ Church, Cockfosters**, at the far end of the Piccadilly Line, is another prosperous suburban church but, unlike St Mary's, Barnes, its worship is strongly Evangelical and is typical of many successful outer suburban parishes. The church itself is a stock brick lancet Gothic structure of 1839, now swallowed up by inter-war suburbia, but the parish is prosperous and well appointed. The vicar has three curates – one of whom looks after St Paul's, Hadley Wood – and is also assisted by two licensed lay workers.

Although Evangelical, Christ Church offers many Communion services: regularly at 9.30 a.m. on a Sunday, at which the ASB alternates with the 1662 words, and also sometimes at 8.00 a.m. or 12.15 p.m. On February 5th, 1984, the 11 o'clock service was the Family Service which takes place once a month. This employs a special family worship service book which is designed, presumably, for children. This provides for such events as a 'Singalong: There will either be a special item or we shall sing together', and an 'Illustrated Talk' rather than a sermon, as well as special prayers for those who particularly need them, such as teachers, who 'need your guidance as they plan their lessons', and 'Writers, Radio, Television, etc.'

The Family Service is very popular. People were arriving a quarter of an hour before 11 o'clock to secure a good seat and eventually over three hundred were present. Many were young married couples with children, but there were older parishioners as well. There was a strong emphasis on participation and on explaining the significance of things to the children. Prayers and readings were led by members of the laity. Steve and Sue (apparently obligatory Evangelical names: see St Mary's, Islington, above) read from two books they commended to those present: *Let's Pray Together* and *The All Colour Book of Bible Stories*. Then came the 'Singalong', which was a repeat performance of songs from *Kids' Praise* led by a man with a beard, in which the children sang biblical texts to the accompaniment of a tape-recorder playing Afro-Caribbean rhythms rather than music of the European tradition.

Awards were then given for Sunday School attendance; Dominic Belisario taking the prize for a hundred attendances. Then came the collection, during which music was played by an orchestra placed in the chancel. This was difficult as the chancel was occupied by not only bulky electronic amplification equipment but also an epidiascope and a screen. These last were needed for the 'Illustrated Talk'. One of the curates delivered a sermon on the theme of the Lost Sheep, which was illustrated by drawings of 'Cedric the Sheep' projected on the screen. This was followed by children asking questions.

Clearly the church was too small and ill-equipped to contain the various activities which took place in the parish.

It was therefore no surprise to find plans pinned up at the back of the church showing the proposed extension, labelled 'Lounge', which will contain proper audio-visual facilities. This will require building over much of the churchyard, at present full of tombs and gravestones, which contributes to the village atmosphere which this part of Cockfosters still enjoys, and despite the fact that Christ Church has its own church hall near by. Most of the rest of the churchyard is to be tarmacadamed as a car park. There seems little sense of reverence in Cockfosters, either inside or outside Christ Church.

That evening the Evening Service was to include a showing of a film, 'Mission to London', about the mission of Luis Palau, the Argentinian evangelist, in London, planned for the following June. Christ Church, Cockfosters, was involved in this campaign, even though this suburb seems utterly remote from the problems faced by the church in central London.

Indeed, the contrast not only in means but in attitude and worship between suburban and urban Anglicanism can be so extreme as to be painful. Extreme contrasts can also exist within the same area, as is shown in Deptford, one of the poorest and most deprived parts of South-East London. Deptford is beset by the problems of the inner city – poverty, decay, race, indifference, vandalism – about which Anglican bishops say they are so deeply concerned.

**St Luke's, Deptford**, is a heavy, ragstone Gothic church of 1870 in Evelyn Street – a main road surrounded by drab post-war housing estates. Its parish is now united with that of the old church of St Nicholas, rebuilt in the late seventeenth century, where a service had been held at 10 o'clock on February 12th, 1984. The 11 o'clock service at St Luke's was described as Morning Prayer, but it was difficult at first for the visitor to appreciate quite what was going on. Entering by the North transept, I found a reordered centralised space with a modern wooden altar table placed opposite in the former South transept, while the apse and former chancel were filled with seats. The nave had been sealed off as a separate space and the new partition was decorated with a red banner proclaiming 'Joy in the City'. There was also an organ placed against this wall but this instrument was redundant.

When I arrived (late) I felt as if I had intruded into a private party. The atmosphere was that of Sunday School. In front of the altar a layman was telling stories to children who were being encouraged to ask questions and to plant trees in toy boxes of earth on the floor. The congregation, meanwhile, was singing 'The Wise Man built his House upon the Rock' to a jaunty tune reminiscent of the days of skiffle-groups and played by two female guitarists and a bearded pianist. I looked for the clergy. They were in evidence; one sitting behind the altar in a white alb was cheerfully singing and laughing. This was the vicar.

Tree-planting was followed by a moral tale on the theme of 'Where is your heart?' First the lesson – about motes and beams in the eye, or, rather, specks and boards – was read by a youth, very badly, out of a paperback Good News Bible. To make the meaning clear a mime was then acted by one of the clergy, with his 'heart', represented by a girl at the end of a piece of string, wearing a large red heart-shaped cushion tied to her stomach. Then followed more singing, with the congregation waving their hands in the air – 'Clap your hands, clap your hands/Sing unto the Lord give all you can . . .' The Lord's Prayer was also sung, to a 1960s-style country-'n-western rhythm, accompanied by the guitarists and a flute-playing clergyman.

Then followed a baptism, for which the congregation gathered in the centre of the church. After the godparents of the child, Lee, had repeated their baptismal vows (according to the Series 2 rite), the vicar replied 'Terrific! . . . Right! Now we're getting on!' and led the proceedings with genuine gusto and enthusiasm. Finally came the

Blessing – 'May you have peace and be touched by life!' – delivered in front of a semicircle of Brownies who had received back their flags.

It is difficult to know how to react to such a service, as this sort of religion is clearly popular. The congregation numbered about eighty, with white and black, young and old all happy to sing along and wave their hands in the air. The vicar had been there for ten years, but felt that only in the previous fifteen months, since he had popularised the worship, was he achieving anything. Local people found conventional services 'boring', and what mattered in a place like Deptford was getting at people's hearts through 'communication'. Despite all the emotion and spontaneous gestures, the service did in fact have a conventional structure and used the language of Series 2. The danger must surely be that those who grow up in such a religious environment will associate Christianity with community events, play-acting and dated 1950s popular music. There seemed to be little contact with the great traditions of Anglicanism, nor was there any atmosphere of reverence or dignity.

That it is possible to combine community activities and social concern with a dignified liturgy and the proper use of a grand, traditional church building is suggested by **St Paul's, Deptford**, just half a mile away. But whereas St Luke's is very Evangelical, St Paul's is very 'high'. Designed by Thomas Archer, St Paul's is one of the great masterpieces of the English baroque. It is precisely the type of monumental and historical church building that the Church of England has condemned as redundant in recent years. In Deptford, however, St Paul's is one of the very few visible symbols of continuity when so much of the area has been devastated and rebuilt. This the rector, Fr David Diamond, well appreciates and, as he wrote in an appeal booklet, *Down Deptford Way*, in 1973, 'St Paul's is not only revered as a legacy of the past, but as a building of immense character and beauty to be restored for the future. As the new "clinical" estates grow around her – so much more is the building appreciated. Today, more than ever, we *need* our "Mounts of Transfiguration" if we are to serve the community.' Such optimism was fully justified and the building has been magnificently restored.

David Diamond came to Deptford from St John's, Tue Brook, Liverpool, in 1969. St Paul's then seemed utterly remote from the people of Deptford. The services were '1662 with incense' and the congregations about half a dozen in size. With the help of two curates, Fr Diamond set about reviving the parish:

> . . . the next move was to go out into the community to build a personal bridge across the gaping chasm that separated the Church from this artisan town. Before long the clergy were frequently seen in the local pubs; chatting to teenagers on the street corners; attending meetings of tenants' associations; speaking for defendants in court . . .

The creation of the Deptford festival in 1970 helped make St Paul's the centre of local life again. Fr Diamond's model has been Fr Dolling, vicar of St Agatha's Landport, in the Portsmouth dockyards in the 1890s, who believed that, 'Since the Reformation, the Church of England has been lost to the masses; it is a church which, whatever its excellences in other directions, has been out of touch with the interests and ideas of the "common people" of England.' Fr Diamond's answer was not to compromise the faith but to emphasise the Incarnation within the Prayer Book tradition. He feels he has more in common with the Roman Catholics over the road than with the Evangelicals at St Luke's.

The success of this approach can be seen today. At the 10 o'clock People's Mass on February 19th, 1984, there was a congregation of over a hundred, mixed in age, sex and race. There was an atmosphere of friendly familiarity with the form of service. Hymn numbers were announced by a (black) churchwarden at the back of the church, but this did not affect the dignity of the ceremonial. There were three vested priests, two servers and two little black acolytes. A forward altar was used in the shallow apsidal sanctuary so that the architectural integrity of Archer's centralised design was in no way impaired. The service was, in fact, old-fashioned High Church, using the words of the Prayer Book with proper ceremonial. At the end, a newly-baptised child was welcomed into the church by being sprinkled with holy water at the altar rails. All was done in a matter-of-fact dignified manner, and nothing was arch or camp.

It was a little sad, therefore, to learn that changes were planned. Even though this traditional form of service worked, the clergy seemed anxious to use the new Roman missal. This upset the middle-class elements of the congregation, who come from Greenwich and Blackheath, but a local lady thought there was no point in using a language in church which nobody speaks today. After the service, coffee was served in the crypt which, cleared of its bodies, now serves many functions for local people: reggae on Fridays for the black population; a discothèque for whites on Saturdays. The majority of the congregation are just the same in composition or class as those at St Luke's, Deptford, but the way the building and the traditions of Anglicanism are used could not be more different.

St Paul's also is in marked contrast to the policies adopted by the Church of England in the most notorious of inner-city areas with racial problems: Brixton. **St Matthew's, Brixton**, is one of the four large 'Waterloo Churches' built in the 1820s in South London. Designed by C. F. Porden, it is a large Greek Revival building of stone, with portico and steeple, on a commanding and open site. Today the surroundings are ill-kept and the church looks closed. Among various posters on the wire fencing, there was no notice advertising Anglican church services. To enter the building brings no further enlightenment, for the interior of the church has disappeared. Behind the portico is a raw concrete space, reminiscent of an underground car park. In the centre of this is a giant, circular concrete lift-shaft. Either side of this are small doors, the wire glass windows of which reveal that there is a room behind filled with plastic stacking chairs. This is St Matthew's Church, Brixton. The crypt below has been converted for other purposes while above this 'worship centre' a theatre has been constructed.

The Church of England no longer has any visible and recognisable presence in Brixton. Most people think Porden's monumental building is a dance studio. There were until recently five churches in Brixton. Three have been sold, St Matthew's converted to a multiple-use community centre and St John's, Angell Town, a ragstone Gothic building with a tower, is falling down. In 1977, with the encouragement of the diocese of Southwark, the parish church council decided to convert the interior of St Matthew's and to lease the building to a community trust for ninety-nine years. The result is that the parishioners feel that the church no longer belongs to them and the parish only has one vote out of seventeen in the management committee.

About forty people, mostly black, were present in the back room for the Sung Eucharist on December 11th, 1983. The singing was powerful and enthusiastic, but there was something forlorn and depressing about this service held in a hideous room in the back of a rather brutally designed community centre. The living was vacant at the time and the celebrant was one of the two curates who admitted, afterwards, that the whole scheme had been a disaster. He seemed sour and bitter about what had happened and said he would oppose the conversion if it was proposed again. The scheme had been pushed through by the 'white trendies who dominate the PCC' using the excuse of the community needs of the blacks to get their way. But the local blacks saw the exercise as yet another example of white oppression, and the inhabitants of the nearby housing estate, who need a community centre, feel that St Matthew's is now denied to them as an accessible building. The congregation was now declining as the black members did not like the change, while for the former old white congregation it was 'dead'.

The case of St Matthew's, Brixton, shows that so much of the progressive posturing of the modern Church of England can end in the betrayal of both past and future and an acceleration of the decline of inner-urban Anglicanism. The disillusioned curate has now gone to the **St Paul's** area of **Bristol**, where the Church's response to a racially mixed urban society can also be studied. St Paul's achieved notoriety during the riots of 1970. The area takes its name from the eponymous church, a handsome and pretty Georgian Gothic building of the 1790s. Despite its architectural quality and importance in Portland Square, and despite the problems of the area, St Paul's was still proposed for redundancy in 1982. Fortunately, with the local authority's spending money on the district, St Paul's has become united with three other parishes. St Agnes' and St Werburgh's are still used for worship while St Barnabas's Church has been demolished and the vicarage is used as a parish centre. These united parishes are now run by a team ministry of three priests – one non-stipendiary – and a deaconess.

On July 15th, 1984, the Family Eucharist at 11.15 a.m. at St Paul's was taken by Fr Charles, a cheerful Barbadian who is a bus driver during the week. The congregation numbered twenty-two with three old (white) ladies and eleven (black) children and the majority black. St Paul's used to have a conservative Evangelical tradition of worship and Fr Charles was clearly unfamiliar with the Series 1 & 2 service book as nothing seemed to happen in quite the right place. The Kiss of Peace was celebrated with enthusiasm and children screamed. The sermon was delivered by Deaconess Bernice who, dismayed by the smallness of the congregation, announced that she would abandon her prepared text and expressed the hope that, as the week was Pentecost 5, the Spirit would move her. Her theme was the Church's mission to all men and she talked of the difficulty of abandoning established places and traditions – as she had experienced herself when coming to Bristol from Newcastle. She also spoke of the necessity of bridging gaps, as between Anglo-Catholics and Evangelicals. This was certainly happening at St Paul's.

**St Agnes'**, a pink ragstone mid-Victorian church next to a 'Tupperware Centre' a few streets away, had an Anglo-Catholic tradition but, as an old, white member of the congregation remarked, with the team ministry the different churches were 'coming closer together now'. The 9.30 a.m. Sung Eucharist on the same day attracted a congregation of about forty, some half of whom were black and with fewer, and quieter, children than at St Paul's. All was very friendly and coffee was served in the north aisle after the service, but, to judge by the notice-board, the parish is deeply committed to racial politics. But in the churches in St Paul's, Bristol, the Church of England seems to be successful in promoting racial harmony.

The uniting of parishes can often work in cities because the resulting large parish can still be a coherent unit. There is a long tradition of centralised team ministries in cities, as can be seen in Portsmouth and Leeds (discussed below). The merging of parishes is more common in the country, however, as a solution to the problem of many village churches with small congregations. In such cases there is no team ministry, only one clergyman who may have to look after four or five churches and who spends his Sundays driving furiously from one to another to take services. The result is that in many parts of the country, such as Norfolk, villages have lost their vicar and their rectory, the church is no longer a vital centre of local life and is only open, perhaps as little as once a month, for a service. This state of affairs has undoubtedly been responsible for the decline in church attendance in rural areas which is quite as conspicuous as the decline in urban areas.

**Hedgerley** is a Buckinghamshire village near Beaconsfield. Even though it is near London and has a rising population, – 60 per cent of the villagers are council tenants – the village now has to share an incumbent with the neighbouring villages of Farnham Common and Farnham Royal. The rectory, a small and very desirable house of the 1840s, has been sold. The rector, who lives in Farnham Royal four miles away, claims about £6,000 a year from the diocese in travel expenses – almost enough, as he points out, to employ another clergyman. In fact he feels that Hedgerley Church – a Victorian rebuild of a much older structure – could run without him as he is assisted by a retired canon and a non-stipendiary curate – a chemist from Farnham Royal – and because the village is a very cohesive and loyal community. He is lucky, for this is not the case in many rural areas.

For Morning Service at 11 o'clock on January 8th, 1984, there were twenty-eight people in church, all villagers in their Sunday best, and a choir of seven girls and one man. The Book of Common Prayer was used, with variations, although its effect was reduced by the use of the *Psalm Praise* book. On every other Sunday the Alternative Service Book is used for Holy Communion.

**Weobley**, in Herefordshire, is fortunate in still having a vicar and a vicarage – at present. The church is essentially mediaeval with a particularly splendid steeple, and is clearly important to the village because in 1982 £14,000 was raised locally to replace and rehang the bells. On most Sundays, Series 3 is used in church, but, on July 31st, 1983, as it was the fifth Sunday in the month, the Book of Common Prayer was retained for the 11 o'clock Holy Communion. Presumably this concession to older villagers was made because the 1662 words are loved and familiar. Even so, the vicar managed to ruin the effect by redundantly calling out the page numbers – something which seems obligatory in many country churches and which breaks any flow and continuity in the service.

There was a congregation of about forty villagers, mixed in age and sex. There was also a choir of eleven, almost all women and all dressed in uniform. This choir processed self-importantly up the aisle but, in fact, contributed little to the singing. The vicar's wife read the epistle. The vicar's sermon, on the subject of 'service' to God and to the community, was rambling and patronising and distinguished by a complete misunderstanding of the Parable of the Talents. He seemed more enthusiastic about the notices as they were mostly about Tanzania, where he had acquired his experience as a missionary, a fact which apparently informs the majority of his sermons. All these proceedings were conducted in the nave of the church; the chancel was used only for Holy Communion. The whole service was dull, ramshackle and somehow irreverent.

A year later, in July 1984, the 11 o'clock Family Service was not held in the church, built centuries before and consecrated for divine worship, but on the vicarage lawn. This was because it was a sunny day. As it was hot, the church cool and I dislike sitting on lawns, I could not bring myself to attend this gathering. The following report of it appeared in the parish newsletter:

The sun shone down on the service which was presented by the After Eights under the direction of Hugh Disley, who began by telling us that outdoor services reminded him of the many services held in the open in Tanzania. The theme was 'What kind of Christian am I?' and was full of music, prayer and comic sketches, some written by the After Eights on the Saturday in their workshop. The children sitting on the grass were enthralled throughout and the whole service was a very pleasurable experience.

What those villagers who like their worship to have the structure required by law of the Church of England and who like their parish church used for its proper purpose thought of this open-air conviviality was not recorded. At least it demonstrated the usefulness of the vicarage, of which the vicar is anxious to dispose. His wife finds this substantial Georgian house too big and so, regardless of the unhappiness felt about this in the village and of the needs and wishes of her successor, a new vicarage is to be built next door.

Dull, complacent, cosy services combined with the baring of middle-class guilt about the Third World is not, however, confined to country churches. It can happen in towns. **All Saints', Hastings**, is a mediaeval church on the edge of the old town. The congregation use this building and St Clement's, another mediaeval church, alternately. At the parish Communion at 10.30 a.m. on January 22nd, 1984, there were about ninety present, largely middle-aged and middle-class. The vicar and his curate presided, together with a choir of fourteen and two women in dressing-gowns: one in black and one mulberry-coloured. Both ladies served the chalice at Communion. The Rite A of the Alternative Service Book was used, the whole service was vaguely 'high' and cosy and the Peace was celebrated with particular enthusiasm.

The sermon, delivered by the curate, on the Feeding of the Five Thousand, dwelt on the theme of Christ's caring for people: 'You poor darlings! You must be hungry . . .' The disclaimer, 'I hope I won't be accused of being political if I say . . .' was a prelude to a moral discourse on the sins of Britain and its duties to the Third World. The congregation may, or may not, have been pleased to be told that 'Elitism is contrary to the teachings of Christ' and that only the poor can enter the Kingdom of God, because few of them were poor, but most regular church-going Anglicans are probably used to being told that they are the least worthy members of the human race. The real reason for the curate's enthusiasm for the Third World soon emerged, however, for he had spent some time in Papua New Guinea which was 'really a continuous learning experience' and where it was 'wonderful to feel strong brown hands clasping around my waist from behind' while crossing rope-bridges. This embrace seems to have implanted the not necessarily Christian conviction in the curate that Britain should simply be a soup-kitchen to the rest of the world.

It is, nevertheless, possible to hear an intelligent, witty and profound sermon from an Anglican pulpit. The pulpit at **Holy Trinity, Reading**, is a high one in every sense. The vicar, Fr Brian Brindley, is one of the most conspicuous and flamboyant clergymen in the Church of England, and he has enlivened a dull Gothic box of the 1820s with splendid furniture thrown out of other churches. There is Pugin's screen from the Roman Catholic cathedral in Birmingham straddling the building, while the pulpit is huge and Georgian, complete with sounding-board, taken from All Saints', Oxford (since converted into a library). This beautification, combined with the impeccably performed ceremonial and excellent music, has attracted a loyal congregation and the church is full of life. Services are advertised in the *Church Times* where convenient train times from Paddington are also given. Naturally the tradition of the church is extreme Anglo-Catholic; the 'Missa Normativa' is used and this is one of the few Romanising churches left – both in the Anglican and Roman Catholic churches – where birettas are still worn (for a portrait of Fr Brindley, see the *Tatler* of January 1985).

There was a congregation of about fifty present for the parish Mass at 11 o'clock on July 17th, 1983. Many, but by no means all of these were elegant, youngish men. There was also a (male) choir of seven and four servers. Priest, curate and deacon were all fully vested. The sermon, delivered by Fr Brindley from his magnificent pulpit, was concerned with the 150th anniversary of the Oxford Movement which had been celebrated the day before in Oxford by the Archbishop of Canterbury at an open-air service. The sermon was suitably optimistic – Fr Brindley looked forward to meeting the congregation again in fifty years' time to celebrate the 200th birthday of the Movement – and serious. Considering that 'the Church of England is as beyond hope of improvement now as in 1833', he discussed the positive attributes of the heroes of the Oxford Movement: Froude, 'extravagance and joy'; Newman 'integrity'; Keble, 'sweetness'; and Pusey, 'firmness'.

In his eccentricity, of course, Fr Brindley is supremely Anglican. He shows how unorthodoxy can be positive and not negative, creative rather than destructive. Holy Trinity is a centre of ritual and of tradition, which is clearly appreciated and therefore needed. Although he believes that both the Oxford Movement and his ceremonial are 'a gesture of defiance to the stodginess of the Church of England', he does not become a Roman Catholic. He could exist only within the Church of England. But he has been in Reading for eighteen years: a man of such talent, intelligence and style could surely achieve much elsewhere. But he is offered no preferment: he is too extreme.

**St Mary's, Portsea**, is not at all extreme. It is a supremely representative and highly successful Anglican church for it has been the training-ground of bishops and archbishops. Cosmo Gordon Lang and Cyril Garbett, later Archbishops of Canterbury and York respectively, were both formerly vicars of Portsea. For a century St Mary's has been a model for parish organisation and activity in urban areas. It was not the first but remains one of the best examples of a large parish containing several associated mission churches with a team of clergy working together. As rural Portsea became swallowed up by the growth of Portsmouth, the vicar of Portsea in the 1880s, Edgar Jacob, decided on this policy rather than to allow the creation of new small parishes. As he wrote,

> It has been found in London and elsewhere that sub-division of large working-class parishes has not proved an entire success, that the large staff of associated clergy, working from a common centre with mission buildings all round, is a more effective way of reaching people and promoting unity.

Lang, who was at Portsea from 1896 until 1901, 'always considered that the years – say 1890 to 1914 – were the Golden Age of parochial work in the towns of England.' In the years before the 1914–18 war, under Garbett, St Mary's had sixteen assistant clergy. The population of the parish then was over 40,000. Today it is 20,000 and the vicar of Portsea has five assistants. There are still mission churches, but the number has been reduced. Some were bombed and in the 1960s seven churches were reduced to two: St Faith's and St Wilfrid's. The St Mary's church hall, a substantial building, has been leased to Radio Victory, but the parish remains vigorous and active.

Edgar Jacob was responsible for building the present St Mary's, the third church on the site and a building of cathedral size. Indeed, many felt that St Mary's should have become Portsmouth Cathedral rather than St Thomas's, which stands, a little forlornly, near the harbour. Designed by Arthur Blomfield, St Mary's was opened in 1889. Late Gothic in style and reminiscent of East Anglian churches, it has a tall West tower which remains a local landmark. Jacob wrote:

> There it stands as the silent witness for God. It is more eloquent than the lips of any man. The most beautiful public building in Portsmouth is now a building avowedly raised to the glory of

God, testifying in an age of wonderful material progress to the reality of men's belief in a spiritual world, and challenging attention to the question of all questions: 'What think ye of Christ?' This great church of ours will and must be either a means of purifying and blessing the parish or the very monument of its spiritual ruin.

Jacob's optimism remains justified. St Mary's continues to be at the centre of Portsmouth life, at least to judge by the fact that local people are anxious to be married in it. There are 120–130 weddings there a year.

On November 13th, 1983, there was a congregation of nearly 150 at the 10 o'clock Family Eucharist which included both a phalanx of old ladies and many noisy children. A Sunday School of about twenty children entered in the middle of the service and there was a large choir of over twenty men and boys. St Mary's has been 'high' since the 1920s and the vicar and three curates concelebrated. Rite A of the ASB was used. This was Remembrance Sunday, but no mention of this was made in the sermon which was given by one of the curates and which explored the curious metaphor that the Body of Christ was like a wire mesh fence, allowing the Holy Spirit to 'breeze through'. A separate Remembrance Sunday service was held at 3 o'clock in the afternoon at which the civic importance of St Mary's, Portsea, was evident. The church was full with regular parishioners, Scouts, Guides and the British Legion.

A great contrast with St Mary's is presented by **St Faith's Mission, Landport**, one of the two surviving mission churches within the parish. The old mission buildings were damaged in the war and new ones were erected in 1956–7. They consist of a church, which, though typically mean in appearance for the date, is still clearly a church building, and the St Faith's Centre, a complex of rooms and halls, much used by local people for weddings, parties, music practice, karate, and suchlike. The curate-in-charge now has a house immediately next to the church, which has an average congregation of forty to fifty on a Sunday and about ten baptisms a year.

When the mission was first established in 1879 it was built among tightly-packed terraced houses. Today it is surrounded by bleak post-war council housing, but this does not mean that the social problems present in the late nineteenth century – criminality, drunkenness, prostitution – have been eradicated. As the previous curate-in-charge, Michael Sparrow, wrote in his centenary history of the mission,

> In one sense Landport is in a worse situation than it was at the end of the last century. For then the (now much maligned) Victorian social and religious conscience was sending money and workers into the district. Today when faith is weak and mission no more than a memory, the tendency is for the Church to withdraw from this type of area, to hand over its buildings to other agencies, and to leave the authorities of city and county to affect any improvement in Landport, and it is clear that they are not solving the problems . . . Today, when the Church is looking for a way forward in the inner city, this great parish has a new opportunity to assist in that search. We believe that St Faith's Mission, with its fine heritage, with the dedication and hard work of its people, and with its vigorous but reverent tradition of worship, has its own special contribution to make to the variety of ministries within our parish, and to an understanding of their place within a missionary parochial strategy.

Being essentially an island, Portsmouth remains an untypical place with a high proportion of churches still working and a high level of church attendance compared with the rest of the country. It is very different from Hull, the collapsed and depressed Yorkshire port at the mouth of the Humber. According to a report issued in 1980 by the Nationwide Initiative in Evangelism, entitled *Prospect for the Eighties*, North Humberside has the lowest figure for church attendance in the country with only 7 per cent of the population being church-goers of any denomination. And North Humberside also comprises Beverley, with its two great mediaeval churches: the Minster and St Mary's. The Church of England certainly does not loom large in Hull. Although the mediaeval parish church is the oldest and most impressive building in the old town and still gives identity to a much ravaged urban area, many other Victorian churches have been demolished since the Second World War and their parishes united.

The church of **St Stephen The Martyr, Sculcoates**, in Spring Bank about half a mile from the centre of the city, serves three former parishes. A supermarket now stands on the site of one of the old churches while All Saints', Margaret Street, Sculcoates, a fine building by G. E. Street, was demolished in the 1970s. The building which is now intended to cater for the spiritual needs of this large and populous inner-city parish was not even built as an Anglican church. It is a Methodist chapel, erected in 1958, of mean and miserable appearance, which makes no impact whatever in the neighbourhood. Older Methodist churches are more dominant. This chapel was purchased and consecrated as an Anglican church in 1972.

The present incumbent, the Rev F. A. C. S. Bown, has done his best to make a silk purse out of this sow's ear. An altar bearing six baroque candlesticks and a tabernacle has been placed against the East wall to create a sanctuary, while two chapels have been made within the glazed porch. Hull is traditionally Low Church; St Stephen's is extreme Anglo-Catholic. Fr Bown is conservative and the liturgy used is from what is properly called the 'English missal', that is the translation of the old Roman missal combined with bits from the Book of Common Prayer which was made by Fr Kenrick and published in 1933. This was the standard Anglo-Catholic rite before Vatican II. High Mass on Sunday is preceded by the Asperges and concluded with

the Angelus. The biretta is worn. At the 9.30 a.m. High
Mass on July 3rd, 1983, there was a congregation of sixteen
in church, excluding three servers and an organist. Three-
quarters of the congregation were women over the age of
50. The service was conducted with all possible dignity and
reverence.

It cannot, of course, be claimed that St Stephen's, Hull, is
in any way typical even of the Anglo-Catholic wing of the
Church of England, for Fr Bown is the chairman of *Ecclesia*,
the society which defends Tridentine Catholicism within
the Anglican tradition, and is notorious in the pages of the
*Church Times* for his firm stand on such issues as women
priests and abortion. (Possibly, he courts publicity: a long
account of his life and struggles by the present writer was
published in the *Tatler* in January 1985.) On Saturday, July
2nd, 1983, at 8 o'clock in the morning a requiem Mass was
said at St Stephen's for Bishop Carmino da Catanzaro of the
schismatic Continuing Anglican Church in Canada, which
is implacably opposed to the ordination of women. There
was a congregation of three (only one a parishioner). But in
Hull, given the miserable and ineffective 'plant' provided
by the diocese, it seems doubtful if any other tradition of
worship could make much more impact on an inert and
depressing area. It also seems foolish that the vicarage in a
substantial terraced house in Westbourne Park is almost a
mile away from the church.

The state of affairs in Hull parish church was not much
more encouraging. **Holy Trinity, Hull,** is a late mediaeval
building of great size and dignity, standing by the market-
place between the commercial city centre and the derelict
and depopulated area by the Humber. With few people
living within its immediate parish boundaries, this noble
church must obviously draw its congregation from the
whole city. Unfortunately, Holy Trinity, which has the
largest floor area of any parish church in England, looked
rather empty on July 3rd, 1983, when about forty people

were sitting in the early Victorian pews with their tall poppy-head ends for the 10.30 a.m. parish Communion.

Holy Trinity has an emphatic and old-fashioned Low Church tradition. Parish Communion is only celebrated on the first Sunday of the month. There was a surpliced choir of about eighteen men and boys. The vicar wore surplice and hood. The curate, who wore a moustache, informed the congregation of the relevant page numbers in the Alternative Service Book. The congregation was mixed in both age and sex. The vicar, the Rev J. Dawson, gave a long sermon, the chief theme of which was the need for the laity to involve themselves more in the life of the Church. Holy Trinity, he said, needed to be run with the efficiency and good management expected in business. The collection was given to the Society for the Conversion of the Jews. In conclusion he commended to the congregation the enthusiasm of his children as they shouted a catch-phrase they had picked up from television. 'This should be our motto in this church – Sock it!' But the congregation looked unimpressed and rather unlikely to sock anything to anybody. Why should they? Although the liturgy was dull and perfunctory, the great merit of Holy Trinity is that it is there, somehow transcending the drab and depressing reality of modern Hull. The building has not yet been spoiled; it may well come into its own again in the future.

The Church of England seems rather more healthy in the Yorkshire city of **Leeds**, where there is a general High Church tradition stemming from the vigorous activity of Dean Hook, Vicar of Leeds from 1837 to 1859. Bad mistakes have been made: many churches and the wrong churches have been closed in Leeds in recent years, although not as many, proportionately, as in Hull or Liverpool. Unfortunately, it was decided to close the oldest surviving church in Leeds, the early seventeenth-century church of St John, in New Briggate, which is one of the most interesting churches of its date in the country. It is now preserved by the Redundant Churches Fund. The survival of Holy Trinity, a Georgian church with a Low Church tradition right in the centre of Leeds and now surrounded by a shopping centre, seems precarious and at one stage it was actually proposed to demolish Leeds Parish Church.

Although, since 1869, cut off from the centre of the city by a tiresome railway which cut through part of the churchyard and now on the fringe of a derelict area, St Peter's, Kirkgate, better known as **Leeds Parish Church**, remains the centre of religious life in Leeds. It was built by Dean Hook in 1838–41 to revive moribund Anglicanism in the city and to replace a mediaeval building, and it was conceived on a grand scale. St Peter's is a large and serious Gothic Revival church complete with capacious and impressive galleries – a feature which the next generation of Gothicists condemned. It was here that Hook established a tradition of choral worship, a tradition which thrives today and which is supported by loyal Anglicans from all over the city. The Parish Church has no immediate parish, so the congregation is gathered from afar. Really the church functions as a cathedral, as the vicar, Canon Jim Richardson, explains in a note to visitors:

> The worship here is 'cathedral-type' worship because Leeds is the only major city without an Anglican Cathedral. Every single day begins with a simple service in the Lady Chapel when we lift the City up to God in our prayers, remembering those on their way to school and work, mums at home, and the sick and the housebound. And every afternoon Choral Evensong is sung, the boy choristers coming straight from their schools, and the men from their place of work. It is the only Parish Church in England where Evensong is sung daily.

At Evensong at 6.30 p.m. on Sunday, June 3rd, 1984, there was a congregation of about fifty which, even though some were scattered in the galleries, made the densely furnished building look comparatively full. The service was traditional and choral (hardly a church in the country seems to have abandoned 1662 for any Alternative Service Book Evensong) and the choir numbered thirty men and boys. The service was dignified but also clearly a popular social event. At 9.15 a.m. the same day only seven people, mostly elderly, came despite heavy rain to attend Holy Communion said to the words of the Prayer Book, but the principal service was the Sung Eucharist at 10.30 a.m. Much goes on within the building. Part of the North aisle has been discreetly converted into a room for having coffee after the service, and during the week several church groups meet there. There are also organ recitals and other musical events during the week, for the church has a master of music as well as a precentor and the vicar.

Leeds Parish Church represents that element of Anglicanism which is so often dismissed or underrated: the quiet unaffected maintenance of tradition to keep the church as a steady, dependable symbol of the importance of religion in the modern world. It is a type of Anglicanism which is not fashionable and far from spectacular, but it is certainly not dead. It suggests that the Church of England has more serious duties than to attract congregations by showy means and to attract publicity. Leeds Parish Church also shows the loyalty there is to traditional forms of worship even in a Northern city like Leeds.

This is evident elsewhere. At **St Chad's, Far Headingley**, a proud Victorian church in a comfortable Northern suburb, thirty-five people braved torrential rain to attend 8 o'clock Holy Communion with the Book of Common Prayer. The service was solid and dignified, and the 1662 words clearly appreciated by the congregation. Not so by the vicar, however, who felt it necessary to apologise for the old-fashioned service at the door afterwards and assured me that at the 9.30 a.m. parish Communion the ASB is used.

He seemed disconcerted to be told that I, like others presumably, had come expressly for the Prayer Book.

Very, very different is the type of worship at **St Matthias, Burley**, a mid-Victorian ragstone church in a suburb to the West of Leeds which has a Charismatic Evangelical tradition. Like many such churches, St Matthias seems to appeal to young middle-class couples with children. The atmosphere is cheerful: perhaps it places no spiritual demands on people. For the 10.30 a.m. Family Eucharist on June 3rd, 1984, over two hundred people were crammed into the building. In the centre, at the crossing, was placed a forward altar with six chalices standing on it (the chancel of the church was entirely redundant). Behind this altar stood the vicar, in surplice and stole, who welcomed everyone to 'our praise and worship' rather in the manner of a TV compère. After an advertisement for details of Billy Graham video tapes available at the back of the church, the service began with the singing of one of the twenty-six hymns on the song-sheet: 'We bring a sacrifice of praise unto the house of the Lord.' This was accompanied by a piano, a tambourine and two guitars, and sung, loud and ecstatically, to a jaunty, vaguely Caribbean tune. It was surprising, especially at the very beginning of the service, to see respectably dressed men, who might have been bank managers, waving their arms in the air and generating an atmosphere of potential communal frenzy. The second hymn was to be found neither on the sheet nor in the hymn-book, but everyone seemed to know it: one line mentioned 'holding up a holy hand' and most in the congregation duly held up their hands. It was all rather embarrassing for a stranger.

In between the singing and other interludes, the service did have a structure, which was that of Rite A of the ASB. But after the epistle, the vicar invited members of the congregation to 'share a testimony with us'. As none was as yet ready to do so, he came out with one of his own. He had

had a dream about a building of stone with a spear placed in one of the joints. Having discussed the significance of this with his wife, he had decided that the building represented the Christian community, bound together with love as the mortar. But the spear showed how Satan could still get in and break down fellowship. Fellowship is important at St Matthias. The regular congregation contains several house groups, each of which publishes a *Weekly Focus*, or report. The *Weekly Focus* of the group consisting of 'Tom, Francis, Annette, Lynda, Andy, Granny, Chris, Elaine, Pauline, Val, Sheilagh, Brian and Christine, John and Lesley', began by reporting how

> God has been speaking to us about the value of fellowship. Perhaps this is because our house group has new leaders and we all felt a little insecure and needed reassurance. During the time when the group waited for the Lord to lead us to topics for the 'Focus', we were given several pictures. These pictures all had the same theme. The theme was that spiritual strength comes from our corporate fellowship and prayer together . . .

As a result of all this fellowship, which seems to be the essence of religious feeling in many Evangelical churches, St Matthias has a jolly, friendly atmosphere which somehow excludes the casual, or shy visitor. But I was unable to see if any reverent feeling was produced by the rest of the long service and I was obliged to miss the sermon by the moustachioed curate for I had to go on to another church.

This was **All Souls', Blackman Lane**, where the worship not only emphasised the differences between Evangelicalism and Anglo-Catholicism but also the chasm between the suburbs and the inner city which exists within the Church of England in Leeds as elsewhere.

All Souls' is a substantial Anglo-Catholic church in part of inner Leeds, north of the University, which has been devastated by clearance and redevelopment with high-rise council housing. Although some older housing survives and the newer blocks are more civilised, the parish has more than a fair share of the usual urban social problems. But although this is an area where the Church should be making a serious effort, it is clear that All Souls' is being allowed to die. At the 11 o'clock Mass on June 3rd, 1984, only the music was in welcome contrast to that at St Matthias by being part of the Western tradition. Otherwise the differences were depressing. There was a congregation of seventeen, largely consisting of old working-class ladies, and a few tattooed youths at the back of the church. The priest wore modern vestments; the curate and five servers and acolytes cottas. An attempt was made to be very Roman: the 'Missa Normativa' was used naturally and communicants stood to receive at the altar rails. The ceremonial should have been dignified; instead it was both camp and ludicrous. For the gospel, an elaborate procession was assembled, but when he reached the lectern the priest realised that the Bible had been forgotten and he had to rush back to fetch it. The kiss of Peace was celebrated in a grossly excessive manner; some present were determined to kiss everybody, but this was not difficult in view of the smallness of the congregation. Afterwards the clergy and friends went off to the All Souls' Club for a drink; no coffee was offered to the loyal ladies who seem to keep this ill-kempt and sad church going.

All Souls' is a scandal. It represents the wilful waste by the diocese of Ripon of its resources and a betrayal of its responsibilities and the traditions it inherits, for All Souls' is no ordinary, dispensable inner-city Victorian church surplus to requirements. It is the Hook Memorial Church, a magnificent building designed by Sir Gilbert Scott and erected by public subscription in 1876–80 as a memorial to the great Vicar of Leeds. What was built is, today, a fine and serviceable piece of ecclesiastical 'plant', for it includes not only a decent, solid church of reasonable size, but a contiguous clergy house and institute. But the grounds are neglected and the clergy house has been let, so that the clergy live in the sort of new Church Commissioners' vicarage which excites the envy of local people who would prefer to be in a new detached suburban house than in a tower block. They would not be jealous if the old clergy house was in use, for people expect the clergy to live in such Victorian buildings and do not aspire to them.

Worst of all, however, is the use of the institute, or Tennant Hall. The parish priest of All Souls', Fr Alan Sanders, was brought in because of his reputed gifts for social work among working-class people. At first he managed to reverse the decline of the congregation of All Souls' but now the decline has resumed, despite the assistance of a curate, Fr Thornburn, brought in from the diocese of Southwark. Fr Thornburn also has the gift of being able to communicate with young working-class males: so much so, in fact, that he has come to the attention of the local police on several occasions and has since been suspended. The two clergymen seemed to think that their mission was exclusively to the working-class youth of the area. A youth club, with a bar, has been created within the hall. At lunchtime and in the evenings this is well used, but few of the drinkers would seem to go to church as a result. Fr Sanders is often to be seen there, wearing filthy jeans and a black T-shirt which exposes the tattoos on his arms and neck which, mercifully, are hidden by vestments in church. The tattoo on his arm is not of a devotional nature but bears the legend 'Homeward Bound'.

The activities of the clergy at All Souls' have provoked such anger and hostility locally as to be reported in the press. In the *Leeds Other Paper* for June 15th, 1984, it was reported that Fr Sanders had evicted the Church of England Children's Society from Tennant Hall, despite the good work it has done in the area. Fr Sanders, as 'Project Leader' of the Society by virtue of his status as Vicar of All Souls', threatened the paid staff of the Society with redundancy. The paper noted how

Things began to go badly wrong when Father Sanders opened his own Youth Club upstairs in the Hall, which had nothing to do with the official project. From the style of this youth club and by various other actions, Father Sanders began to make apparent his disdain for the 'do-goodish' nature of the Children's Society project of which he was leader. For apparently Father Sanders' style is to go among the ruffians of the local community and convert them into his disciples and the ways of the Lord by having a bar in the Youth Club. Others have seen it in a different light – Father Sanders developing his own local mafia.

Such publicity does not further the work of the Church of England. Nor does Fr Sanders's attempt to close St Mark's, Woodhouse Moor, a church with a very different tradition, whose parish is now combined with All Souls'. The PCC of St Mark's, which is anxious to keep the building going, was once told by Fr Sanders that the only time he could see them was at 3.30 *a.m.* Meanwhile All Souls' itself is being neglected and is sometimes left open all night – as a posturing gesture of welcome – and so runs the risk of vandalism or worse. All Souls' is a scandal, but not only of neglect. It is a scandal that the diocese is allowing fine and useful buildings to be misused, the legacies of past benefactors to be betrayed, the reputation of the Church of England to be sullied, and the people of this deprived inner-city district to be denied spiritual care. If things carry on as they are, All Souls' will be a clear candidate for redundancy – but possibly that is what the diocese of Ripon wants.

It is very sad, but not altogether surprising, to have to record that Fr Thornburn fell to his death from the top of a multi-storey car park in Leeds in August 1985, six months after being suspended as curate at All Souls' following his conviction for importuning for immoral purposes in London. The Archdeacon of Leeds has now taken over the management of the parish after irregularities had been discovered in the accounts.

However, on the other side of the city centre, **St Hilda's, Cross Green**, shows that church buildings and an Anglo-Catholic tradition can be used positively in a working-class inner-city district. St Hilda's was originally a mission church within the parish of St Saviour's, Leeds, the pioneer slum church founded by Dr Pusey and opened among the dismal terraces across the River Aire to the East of Leeds Parish Church in 1845. In recent years, owing to the clearance and depopulation of this part of inner Leeds, St Saviour's had been threatened with closure. Now it is run by a priest-in-charge and its parish combined with that of St Hilda's. Although less of a landmark than St Saviour's, St Hilda's is a fine building designed by J. T. Micklethwaite and built in 1876–82. Externally it is of the local red brick and in what Charles Booth once described as the 'bare style', grand and sublime, so often used for churches in slum areas. Internally, it is light, spacious and gorgeous, filled with screens and good fittings.

St Hilda's is renowned for its ceremonial as the high tradition is maintained. The 'Missa Normativa' is used for the 10.30 a.m. parish Mass, but the Book of Common Prayer is retained for Evensong. The average Sunday congregation is eighty, according to the parish priest, Fr Stephen Jones, who does not see his role as a 'community or social worker'. There is no school or club attached to the church, but much goes on in the parish and the building is clearly loved and cared for. Fr Jones also does not find it necessary to shed his cassock for T-shirt and jeans, and he finds the local people want him to be paternalistic and that the laity cannot organise things themselves – a common complaint by the incumbents of working-class parishes. The chief difference between this and the parish of All Souls' is that here the local population are still largely in terraced housing and the parish life has not been wrecked by the dreams of planners. But that alone does not explain the difference between the two parishes in the way that buildings and liturgy, tradition and the ideal of mission promoted by Hook and Pusey are all interpreted.

**Redcar** is a faded seaside resort on the North coast of what used to be the North Riding of Yorkshire. It now mostly consists of housing estates overshadowed by the distant silhouette of the British Steel works towards Middlesbrough, to which Redcar is essentially a dormitory suburb. Redcar is therefore depressed with a high rate of unemployment. The oldest building in Redcar is St Peter's, a Gothic building of 1828–9 by Ignatius Bonomi, near the sea-front. This is in poor structural condition and, although its tower is a landmark, the whole church may be rebuilt.

The oldest church in the area, however, is **St Cuthbert's, Kirkleatham**, a Georgian church by Carr of York in the extraordinary eighteenth-century village built by the Turner family which miraculously survives intact just outside the Northern fringe of the town. Kirkleatham parish originally included much of Redcar, but when the new church, St Hilda's, was built in Redcar housing estates in the 1960s, it was seriously proposed to close St Cuthbert's. Kirkleatham is now looked after by the clergy at St Hilda's and the old church has a loyal and increasing congregation and is popular for weddings because of its rural setting and its age and historical associations. The mausoleum, designed by Gibbs, of Sir William Turner, a great local benefactor, is attached to the church. At a Communion service in 1982, a congregation of about thirty had driven out to the village. The priest accidentally omitted the whole of the canon of the mass, but nobody seemed to notice.

**St Hilda's, Redcar,** was built in 1969–71 on an open green in the centre of a large sprawling housing estate. The architect, Tony Ellison, was largely given a free hand, but was asked to design a building which would be prominent. In this he succeeded. The modern building is a significant local monument and clearly a church. It is also a practical building, circular in plan with a smaller circular extension which can be opened into the body of the church when required. Otherwise, it is partitioned off as the church hall. Throughout, a simple straightforward modern aesthetic is developed. At the 9.30 a.m. Family Communion on July 22nd, 1984, a congregation of almost 130 people, young and old, was crammed into the circular 'nave'. Extra plastic seats were put out, making movement for late-comers difficult. The parish priest – in modern vestments with appliqué coloured patches – was assisted by two lay readers in albs and female acolytes (the curate was looking after Kirkleatham that morning). The worship was modern Anglo-Catholic, using Rite A of the ASB. The atmosphere was friendly and familiar and yet devout – despite the jaunty settings for the singing by Patrick Appleton (published by the Church Light Music Society). The sermon was given by a lay reader. After the service, most of the congregation had tea in the rear circular 'hall'. The vicar was a local man and the congregation all knew each other. The church seems to be doing its job both spiritually and in giving a focus to the community, for the kiss of Peace was redundant and not indulged in by the congregation. St Hilda's seems to represent straightforward, unpretentious modern Anglicanism in both its building and worship.

On the other side of the railway tracks, Coatham is really part of Redcar, but **Christ Church, Coatham**, has its own parish. Like St Hilda's, it has a slightly diluted High Church tradition, using the Series 3 liturgy. On September 18th, 1983, there was a congregation of about forty for the parish Communion together with a choir of eleven men and boys. The vested priest was assisted by a lay deaconess. In his sermon, the vicar dwelt on the subject that obsesses the Church of England: church attendance. The lesson had been the story of the ten lepers, only one of whom came back to thank Jesus for his cure. The vicar concluded from this that the Church would be doing well if it attracted one in ten of the population. He then referred to the Billy Graham crusade then being planned in Cleveland. He was unsympathetic to Billy Graham's type of Christianity but forced to recognise its merits. He thought that 'the churches have got to respond evangelistically' to modern problems and that 'commitment' is most important. A church-goer should be a 'doer', not just a listener, and we must take the best from Evangelicalism. Finally he pointed to the north wall of the 1850s Gothic Revival church with its proud spire. The wall had been recently painted, but the damp kept coming through: 'That's what it's all about really.'

If the Church of England elsewhere was as essentially healthy as it is in distant Redcar, where parish life quietly flourishes, there would be less to worry about. But to see, and hear, if the heart of the old pre-Tractarian Church of England still beats one must go elsewhere in the North Riding to one of the holiest places in England: Whitby. Here, in AD 657, St Hilda founded an abbey and here, seven years later, the celebrated and momentous Synod was held. Today this small port and resort has four Anglican churches, all run by the Rector of Whitby. These include St Hilda's, a sumptuous and proud late Victorian building on Westcliffe, and St Ninian's, an eighteenth-century proprietary chapel which is now Anglo-Catholic and which is still a proprietary chapel; but most important is St Mary's, the old parish church.

Sitting on the high East cliff in its wild, crowded churchyard below the ruins of Whitby Abbey, **St Mary's, Whitby**, is one of the most extraordinary churches in England. It is a mediaeval building, which was much rebuilt in the eighteenth and early nineteenth centuries and, by some miracle, never 'restored' by the Victorians. As a result, its interior is still crammed with box pews and the Cholmley Pew slams across the chancel arch. Matins, on October 7th, 1984, at 10.30 a.m., suggested that the religion in Whitby was in harmony with the building. The church is loyal to the Book of Common Prayer and the occasion emphasised the essential secular, political status of Anglicanism. It was Harvest Festival Sunday and the service was a civic occasion. The fully robed Mayor of Whitby was present with the Lady Mayoress, as was the Town Clerk, in gown and wig, and other councillors and dignitaries. This civic party comprised about half of the total congregation of eighty. All was very formal, as befitted the occasion – 'Will the congregation please be upstanding' for the entry of the mayor – and yet the service had a slightly amateur, ramshackle air, which also seemed authentic and which suited the chaotic Georgian interior.

The rector, Canon Joe C. Penniston, also looked the part in gown and bands, like someone out of a Rowlandson print, but he was not as eccentric as he at first seemed, and sounded. From the top of the three-decker pulpit he delivered the best sermon I can recall hearing and certainly the best of the three Harvest Festival addresses I managed to encounter in 1984 (Harvest Festival seems quite arbitrary in its occurrence). His words were wise, intelligent, thoughtful and Christian, without any cant, hypocrisy or pretentiousness. His theme was the Gospel text from St Luke 19: '. . . reaping where thou hast not sewn, and gathering where thou hast not strawed', which applies to most of us in modern Britain and which ought to make us feel the contrast between the bumper harvest in England – a gift from God – and the famine in Ethiopia. Here was an attitude towards the Third World which was realistic and charitable, not sanctimonious and guilt-ridden. The rector also referred to a fellow Yorkshireman, a man in English public life who, like Adolf Hitler, tells lies over and over again so that people eventually believe them; this was at the time of the miners' strike. He believed that the reverse was also true: that if good is recommended over and over again, people may act upon it. It was our duty to go out and preach the truth about Christ: we who are the inheritors of a tradition, who do nothing ourselves but live on the achievements of others. Our duty is to add to that tradition and pass on the truth to others and fight evil: a most difficult thing.

It was a sermon worthy of the best traditions of the Church of England, but as I left and walked down the two hundred stone steps to the town below, I felt sad. Sad because the future seemed uncertain. Canon Penniston had announced his retirement and the loyal parishioners who lovingly care for that most extraordinary and powerful building knew not if his successor would respect and maintain the traditions of the place. Furthermore, the congregation had been middle-aged and old; there were no young people present who might carry things on. But the rector himself may have had more confidence, for as he had welcomed the mayor and the civic party he said that 'We who are privileged to worship in this historic place are made aware of the indestructibility of our religion . . . In these days it is a tremendous encouragement that on this spot God has been adored since Saxon days.'

The real sadness is how few clergy, archdeacons and bishops, diocesan boards of finance, church administrators and advisers, seem to share that Rector of Whitby's sense of the power and purpose of the Church of England.

\* \* \*

Speaking in Lambeth Palace, in July 1985, at the launching of an appeal for the restoration of the late Victorian wooden cathedral in Georgetown, Guyana, the Archbishop of Canterbury announced that 'I often think that we attach too little importance today to the significance of buildings and of sacred associations.' Such words are rare from the episcopate and apply as much to England as they do to the exotic architectural legacy of Anglicanism in the former outposts of Empire. To judge by their policies towards church buildings in recent decades, neither most individual dioceses nor the Church Commissioners seem to attach much importance to the significance of sacred and historic architecture. Buildings are regarded as secondary, trivial, merely utilitarian or a financial encumbrance, and, though few in the Church seem to know it, this attitude is responsible for one of the most serious problems the Church of England faces today in its relationship with the nation and with a wider public. All over England people see abandoned, mutilated or demolished churches, the legacies of optimism, sacrifice and love, and draw their own conclusions about the real state of the Church.

As the Archbishop of Canterbury realises, buildings have a powerful effect on people, both within and without the Anglican communion. The destruction of familiar, beautiful or ancient landmarks makes parishioners and others extremely angry. Yet, in its increasingly introverted and defeatist obsession with itself at the expense of its wider established responsibilities, the Church persists in regarding church buildings as unimportant. It is surely significant that, in 1983, while the Church Commissioners spent 6 per cent of its income of £114.4 million on 'administration' a mere 1 per cent was spent on church buildings; 61 per cent was very properly spent on clergy stipends but as much as 7 per cent was spent on 'clergy housing', that is, replacing old and usually serviceable vicarages with new houses.

It is not a joke that many clergymen refer to church buildings as so much 'plant', in the language of the chartered accountant. This may now seem a dated cliché but the attitude is widespread. Indeed, there is a wealth of literature available to advise clergymen how to deal with or dispense with old buildings. A typical and tellingly titled example is *Centres for the Servants. Parish Plant Up-dated* by Kenneth White (Grove Liturgical Study No. 4). This booklet begins with such sentiments as 'Propagating the Gospel is difficult enough without the frustration of buildings which hamstring our progress. Holy stones have become millstones', and it is prefaced by part of the enthronement sermon of an earlier Archbishop of Canterbury, Donald

Coggan, delivered in January 1975: 'Our possessions will have to go, including many of those buildings of small historic value which do little more than consume our money and our energies.'

Of course the Church and church buildings have constantly changed and change can stimulate new life. But it can also destroy and the Evangelical indifference to buildings and to formal structures can often be allied to defeatism about maintenance and Philistinism about the legacy of the past. This particular booklet contains much useful advice about reseating and reordering, about dividing off an aisle or a narthex as a 'lounge'. This can be done sensitively and well: not all reorderings are anywhere near as brutal and destructive as that unleashed on St Matthew's, Brixton, as already described. The booklet does also concede that church buildings of all periods, as architecture, have a role to play, but this is qualified by the assertion that 'the rediscovered notion of conservation is often uncritical and sentimental'.

It is here that the problems arise, for the policies pursued by individual parishes or dioceses are often opposed not only by tiresome 'conservationists' but by ordinary parishioners or local people who have, indeed, a sentimental affection for 'their' church. And these problems are greatly exacerbated by the Church's 'ecclesiastical exemption' from statutory planning and historic building legislation. The Church of England – like other denominations – has the freedom to alter a building in ecclesiastical use which is not enjoyed by the private individual or by any secular organisation. This freedom is increasingly challenged by many amenity societies and other outside individuals. On the other hand, the attempt to protect church buildings from ill-advised alteration or rebuilding is greatly resented by parish congregations, or, more usually, by parish church councils, as unwarranted interference in the internal response of a Christian community to its perceived spiritual needs.

There is a paradox and an irony here. With the growing mood of disestablishment and of introverted sectarianism in the Church of England, the wider responsibilities of a church and a church building to its parish are increasingly abandoned. Yet the privileges which the Anglican Christian community enjoys with regard to its buildings stem from the established and once-powerful historical status of the Church of England. Historic building and planning legislation can be regarded as a democratic reflection of the responsibilities of all property owners to society. This is as true of private houses as it is of public buildings. Historically, this legislation may be comparatively new, but it is nevertheless curious that many Anglicans should oppose statutory controls and continue to regard the treatment of churches as a private matter for, above all buildings, churches have always been seen as public property and as belonging to the community at large. The church was once the centre of local life, and in small villages it often remains so and is regarded as such even by non-Anglicans.

It does seem extraordinary that the power of architecture in furthering the work of the Church of England should often be so little regarded by the Church's authorities and members. Buildings exist as a visible symbol of Christianity and as a standing invitation to participate. Very many people are interested in churches, visit them and, possibly, learn from them. Churches do not, of course, just exist for tourists, but even tourists have souls. A report by Max Hanna, *English Churches and Visitors*, published by the English Tourist Board in 1983, revealed that at least 10 million visits a year are made to English churches, half to village churches, and possibly up to £2 million is spent in them. But, as the incumbent of Little Walsingham Church is quoted as appreciating, visits are not just to be encouraged for making money: 'I feel strongly that parish churches have tremendous potential for proclaiming the Christian faith to visitors, who are often impressionable and have time to look and think.'

Sadly, however, not only are so many churches closed because of the danger of theft and vandalism, but the Church itself is often withdrawing from the public realm. Increasingly the Church of England, in particular (although the other churches pursue the same policies), finds itself in conflict with the local community, with the planning authority and with national amenity societies because of the policies it pursues with regard to its buildings and land. These range from internal alterations and the building of extensions to churches in churchyards to the closure and demolition of church buildings. Not all such policies enjoy 'ecclesiastical exemption' from planning law. One which does not is the replacement of rectories and vicarages. This, again, is something which affects a wider community than the active parishioners. The old rectory is often perceived as a semi-public building which belongs to a village and its sale into the private sphere is resented. The whole question of rectories cannot be discussed here; suffice it to say that it is the Philistinism and incompetence of the Church Commissioners' policy over rectories which invites criticism. A large rectory may have a utility which transcends the immediate needs of a modern-minded rector or the trivial desire of his wife for central heating. When sold, Georgian rectories are often soon resold for a large profit – not enjoyed by the Commissioners themselves, who have also spent much money on building an architecturally undistinguished and often very obtrusive new house. The Church Commissioners' Report for 1984 actually condemns the architectural features of a Georgian or Victorian rectory and recommends the building instead of characterless new brick houses of suburban banality.

A typical case has recently arisen in **Saffron Walden** in Essex, where the new rector, the Rev Peter Harlow, chose in April 1985 to move out of the Georgian rectory by the mediaeval parish church and into a distant suburban villa. Seizing the opportunity, the parsonage and glebe department of the diocese of Chelmsford proposed to demolish the rectory together with the parish room, which is partly fifteenth century, and to build six 'town houses' on the site. Although, arguably, good for the efficiency of the parish and the finance of the diocese, this scheme is causing immense bitterness and hostility in the proud and beautiful old town and it scarcely furthers the real work of the Church of England. Sadly, this local row is far from untypical today.

As the rectory has now been listed, the Saffron Walden proposals may well be stopped by the operation of the planning laws, as has happened with another unpopular scheme in the Surrey village of **Chiddingfold**. Here, the rector, the Rev John Nicholls, and his parish church council wished to build a 'vestry extension' in the old churchyard, arguing, in the words of the rector, that 'it is now necessary to provide separate male and female toilets for the increased congregations and church activities.' However, the proposal was opposed not only by the local authority but by many villagers, who considered that money was better spent on the village's church school or the village hall. A public inquiry was held and, in July 1985, the Department of the Environment turned down the parish's planning application. The result is, nevertheless, much local division and bitterness, with the congregation of what is clearly a healthy church feeling resentful of interference and other villagers feeling hostility to the Church. The irony is that while many parishes in the South of England in villages which are essentially dormitory suburbs to London have a great deal of money to spend on altering and enlarging their church, in many other parts of the country and in cities the congregations have to struggle to keep their existing building in repair.

In Chiddingfold, because the proposed change was external, it required planning permission. The alterations planned for **St Mary's, Bletchley**, near Milton Keynes, were internal and therefore merely required the permission of the diocese. The alterations were, however, so far-

reaching as to change completely the character of the
mediaeval building, and they provoked such opposition as
to be reported widely in the local press (the *Gazette*, October
26th, November 2nd and 9th, 1984). The existing pulpit and
choir-stalls were to be thrown out and new chairs grouped
in circles radiating from a new *octagonal* altar placed at
the side of the nave, thus denying the architectural and
historical logic of the plan of the existing building. The
plans were approved by the parochial church council,
commended by the diocesan advisory committee as 'excit-
ing and imaginative' and executed early in 1985. Some
parishioners, however, called the rector's proposals
'acts of desecration' and several wrote to the local paper
complaining of

> the total lack of concern and empathy shown by the Rector and
> members of the Parochial Church Council towards the older
> members of the congregation who have given substantial
> financial support and service to the church over many years
> . . . The church belongs to the people and is there to administer
> the basic services of baptism, marriage and burial to all who so
> require them. Therefore, the people of this parish should be
> allowed to have their say before any such 're-ordering' takes
> place . . .

The rector, on the other hand, who has the unlikely name of
the Rev Ian Pusey, considered that 'these people, who are
an extreme minority of my parishioners, are talking a load
of rubbish'.

The case of St Mary's, Bletchley, is becoming typical of
Anglican parishes all over the country both in the bitterness
and hostility produced by ruthless change and in the rejection of the Church's traditional social role in favour of
internal preoccupations – one parishioner, an 'accredited
Lay Worker, with a Degree in Theology', wrote to the paper
in support of the proposals as 'We have discovered the
richness and flexibility of the new liturgy. It allows for the

visual communication of the Gospel truths through drama and dance, when occasion demands . . .' It is also typical of the sort of radical internal alteration to a public building which would not be tolerated in the secular sphere without planning permission, and which is bringing 'ecclesiastical exemption' into disrepute. The Church of England's own system of control has been strongly criticised by national conservation and amenity societies, and many within the Church feel that it would be best for the Church of England if it was brought within the scope of the statutory planning laws.

The Church itself has responded to the criticisms by setting up the Faculty Jurisdiction Commission, whose report was published in 1984 for the General Synod under the title *The Continuing Care of Churches and Cathedrals* and the whole question of the reform or abolition of 'ecclesiastical exemption' is now being considered by the Secretary of State for the Environment. (For a lucid discussion of the whole matter, see 'Ecclesiastical Exemption: Church buildings and the law', by John Maddison, in the *Victorian Society Annual 1981*.)

'Ecclesiastical exemption' is an extremely complicated issue and it does not only apply to the Church of England. It stems from the Ancient Monuments Act of 1913 when the Archbishop of Canterbury pleaded that the Church of England was perfectly able to look after its own buildings and did not need the discipline of law. In 1913, when church architecture and restoration was at a high level of sophistication and when most clergymen were reasonably informed on aesthetic matters, this may have been true. It is true no longer and the principal complaint today is that the Church's own system is functioning neither properly nor responsibly. The essence of the system is that all alterations to a church's fabric or its furnishings require a faculty which is issued by the diocese. All such petitions for a faculty come before a diocesan advisory committee (DAC).

A principal complaint against this system is that the

quality of DACs is very uneven. While some, such as that for London, make responsible judgments and include in their composition distinguished experts on church architecture and furnishings, others are primarily concerned with pastoral issues and tend to ignore the claims of architecture and history. The members of DACs are appointed by the bishop and, in the case of Chester and Oxford, in recent years the composition of the DACs has come to be dominated by compliant clergymen. Fortunately, the DAC is not the highest authority. In each diocese there is a consistory court, presided over by a chancellor, or ecclesiastical judge. In the case of **St Mary's, Banbury**, a remarkable Neoclassical church by S. P. Cockerell of 1797, the Oxford DAC approved the plan to remove the box-pews and other furnishings and install a 'movable altar' in the centre of a circular green carpet in the middle of the building. The incumbent, the Rev Ron Mitchison, who used to be part of 'Team V', a team ministry in Banbury, claimed, 'I'm trying to preserve the church not destroy it', while wanting to 'change the church from an old Victorian [sic] relic [sic]' into a 'dynamic new building'. Fortunately, the chancellor of the diocese disagreed and rejected most elements of this destructive scheme early in 1985.

The Victorian Society, like other national amenity societies, argues that if 'ecclesiastical exemption' is to continue, then the system of diocesan advisory committees will have to be reformed. It would like to see several places on these committees reserved for lay representatives of appropriate national or local bodies. The Society's working party on the problem also maintains that

Over the last few years it has become increasingly apparent that the present unsatisfactory state of the law relating to ecclesiastical buildings leads to many disturbing cases. The loophole which permits major parts of churches to be demolished so long as some minor part remains in use for worship has been exploited.

This loophole usually applies to Nonconformist churches, although there are several cases of Anglican churches being rebuilt retaining towers from older buildings. At present, the parochial church council of **St Jude's, Southsea**, a church with a strong Evangelical tradition, wishes to demolish and rebuild the body of the building, leaving only the tower and spire. The vicar, the Rev Tony Turner, proposes to build a block of offices and shops on the site with a comfortable new church attached. The strange and selfish insularity of many modern parishes is shown by the fact that the PCC is determined to go ahead and destroy their building, even though grants are available to cover 50 per cent of the cost of necessary repairs. St Jude's, built in 1851, is essentially sound structurally and an important landmark in Southsea, having been built by, and at the expense of, T. E. Owen, who was responsible for the surrounding housing. There is, therefore, furious local opposition to the parish's proposals, which have scarcely furthered the wider purposes of the Church of England.

A scandalous case of demolition was that of **St Michael's Church, Stourport**, an unfinished building by Sir Gilbert Scott, designed in 1875. After the temporary west end of the church was damaged by a storm in 1976, the vicar, the Rev Patrick Fedden, and his parochial church council decided to demolish the building, even though £15,000 of insurance money was available to repair it. Instead, a new and mean, small church was proposed, to be shared with the United Reformed Church and built on part of the site at a cost of £60,000, with the lower courses of the walls, the porch and a few other features of Scott's building retained as a forecourt. These plans were opposed by a local group which argued that

The demolition of St Michael's and its replacement by a modern building ignores tradition, continuity and the wishes of those who want to see all or much of their existing church retained – including memorials, stained glass windows, an

almost unique Hope-Jones organ and many other fittings of
interest and value.

Twelve parishioners objected to the petition of the vicar and
churchwardens to demolish almost completely the Scott
building and, as a result, a consistory court of the diocese of
Worcester was convened in 1978. A number of national
societies and other witnesses were prepared to give evidence, some arguing that, if necessary, a new church
should be built on another site so that the existing building
could be made redundant and found an alternative use. In
the event, however, the twelve parishioners were obliged
to withdraw for fear of high legal costs and the national
societies were told that they could not be parties to the
action as they were not parishioners. Permission was given
to demolish the building even though the parish did not
have sufficient funds to build anew. Ivor Bulmer-Thomas,
chairman of the Friends of Friendless Churches, commented: 'In the view of the amenity societies it is a severe
condemnation of the procedures of the Church of England
for dealing with its buildings that parishioners are deterred
by the danger of being mulcted in costs from trying to
preserve a church of architectural or historic interest.' In
this case, the local authority approved of the demolition
and the Department of the Environment declined to intervene; even if it had done, and opposed the demolition,
however, the diocese of Worcester and the Stourport PCC
could still have carried on regardless.

The moral and spiritual damage done to the parish of
Stourport-upon-Severn is incalculable. It seems a sorry
comment on the exclusiveness of the modern Church of
England that outside interest in a church building is not so
much welcomed as resented. In far too many cases, the
Church declines to play its traditional social role even
though both local authorities and other interested parties
recognise the problems faced by parishes with large church
buildings and are often anxious to help. Fortunately, there

are examples of the Church co-operating with secular bodies to secure both the preservation of a building and its continuing use both as a church and for the benefit of a wider community – something to which the Church of England, in theory, aspires. In Norfolk, for instance, a county with a sparse population and an embarrassing number of fine mediaeval village churches, the Norfolk Historic Churches Preservation Trust has done much to relieve the Norwich diocese of its responsibilities.

Perhaps one of the most encouraging cases of happy co-operation between the Church and outside voluntary bodies is that of **Christ Church, Spitalfields**. One of the great monuments of the English Baroque, and designed by Hawksmoor, this huge building just East of the City of London was closed in 1957 owing to its structural condition, and the congregation moved to a temporary church a few streets away. Although, in 1965, the roof was repaired with money from the sale of the bombed church of St John's, Smith Square (now restored as a concert hall), and in the same year the crypt was opened as a rehabilitation centre for vagrant alcoholics, it was still proposed to make Christ Church redundant. In the early 1970s, however, volunteers helped to clean the decrepit interior and in 1976 a public concert was held in the building. From this sprang the Friends of Christ Church, Spitalfields, who have raised money from public and private sources to restore it. What is encouraging about this is that the Friends have enjoyed the full co-operation of the rector, the Rev Eddy Stride, who looks forward to moving his congregation back into the church, and it is the intention that the building – which is being restored by the architect Red Mason, of Whitfield Partners, to a higher standard of painstaking historical accuracy than achieved in any of the post-war restorations of City churches – shall serve both as a church and as a concert hall.

In the case of **All Souls', Haley Hill**, a Victorian church was saved from demolition by the action of a voluntary body. All Souls', a proud building in the inner suburbs of Halifax, was built in 1856–9 to the design of Sir Gilbert Scott, who described it as 'on the whole, my best church'. Built by Edward Ackroyd, a local industrialist and philanthropist, it contained excellent stained glass and furniture of its time. By the early 1970s All Souls' had moved from a Broad Church to an Evangelical tradition in worship and the vicar, the Rev Geoffrey Thomas, decided that his building was too much of a burden on his congregation. Services were moved to the church hall over the road, although the abandonment of Scott's building halved the size of the congregation. The diocese of Wakefield was initially opposed to the closure of the church, but it was declared redundant in 1977. By 1980, no alternative use having been found for it and as estimates for necessary repairs approached £500,000, All Souls' seemed doomed. The Advisory Board for Redundant Churches announced, however, that it would oppose demolition and *save* Britain's heritage, and proposed setting up a trust to take on the building and restore it as an ecclesiastical museum. The Friends of All Souls', Haley Hill, were formed in 1981 and the Haley Hill Trust took over the building the following year. A grant of £250,000 from the National Heritage Memorial Fund enabled restoration work to begin.

Instead of decay and demolition announcing to Halifax the abandonment of the Church of England's mission, the building has been saved by courageous outside initiative. What seems absurd is that All Souls' is being restored for a secular purpose while, across the road, the 'Living Church of All Souls' meets in a miserable hut with only crossed neon tubes to announce the existence of a place of worship. It is a powerful and ironic comment on the Church's attitude to sacred architecture, for had the Church's own machinery for redundancy been allowed to pursue its course there is no doubt that decay, vandalism and the huge cost of restoration would have doomed the real All

Souls' which, one day, could be used for worship again.

It is the Church of England's policy of closing redundant churches and demolishing a large proportion of them which has caused the greatest distress and attracted the strongest criticism (see 'Anglican MacGregors', *Spectator*, October 27, 1984, p. 18 and 'The vanishing church of Bishop Jim' concerning the threatened closure of St George's-in-the-East, Stepney, *Spectator*, March 8, 1986, p. 9, both by the present writer). There are, of course, good reasons for declaring churches redundant. Some parts of the country, like Norfolk, are embarrassingly well endowed with village churches or, owing to Victorian munificence and social concern, inner-city parishes may have large churches which poor congregations, depleted by 'urban renewal', cannot maintain. What is conspicuous is that, despite all the talk of the Church's response to inner-city problems, it is the working-class areas of cities which have suffered the most closures. Areas desperately needing an architectural focus and landmark have often been deprived of a monumental church which performed precisely that function. The result is usually disillusionment, bitterness and the disappearance altogether of a Christian presence. While Anglicanism waxes in affluent suburbs, it wanes in the inner-city areas.

What is revealing is that the pattern of church closure varies from diocese to diocese. Few have gone in Truro or Carlisle, yet in Wakefield, since 1968, twelve out of twenty-five redundant churches have been pulled down, and in Liverpool sixteen out of twenty-seven. Some bishops promote 'rationalisation' and the combining of parishes; others do not. What this pattern of redundancies and closure suggests is that there is no such thing, as such, as a redundant church. What there is, often, is a redundant clergyman. The parish of All Souls', Haley Hill, was not redundant; the building was closed owing to the selfish defeatism of a particular incumbent. As the story of All Souls', Leeds, suggests (see p. 193), a bad clergyman can soon make a church redundant, while a good man can revive a parish.

The Church of England established the Pastoral Measure in 1968 to deal with redundant churches. By the end of 1983 1,043 had been closed. Of these 238 have been demolished and 187, considered to be of exceptional architectural quality, have been vested in the Redundant Churches Fund. At the end of 1985 the figure was 1,108. Once a diocese has decided to declare a church redundant, it is very difficult for the parishioners to resist. Indeed, there are very few examples of churches fighting successfully against redundancy. One which did is **Christ Church, Brixton**, an extraordinary neo-Byzantine building, by Beresford Pite, with a strong Evangelical tradition. The churchwardens took their case to the highest authority, the Privy Council, and won. The parish of Christ Church is now combined with that of St John the Divine, Kennington, but is run as an independent church with its own tradition of worship.

In the case of **St Barnabas's, Pimlico**, the churchwardens have so far resisted closure. It seemed extraordinary that such a distinguished church architecturally, and one with such historical importance for the Anglo-Catholic wing of the Church – for it was the scene of the 'Papal Aggression' riots of 1851 – could seriously be proposed for closure. Indeed, this barbarous proposal elicited the last public protest from that great friend of fine churches, Sir John Betjeman.

The principal criticism of the Pastoral Measure concerns both its procedure and, again, the principle of 'ecclesiastical exemption'. Once a church has been declared redundant by a diocese, a three-year 'waiting period' elapses during which an alternative use theoretically is sought. If no suitable use can be found, the Church Commissioners can then decide to demolish the building unless they heed the advice of the Advisory Board for Redundant Churches that it be preserved by the Redundant Churches Fund. It is during the 'waiting period' that the fate of a redundant church is often sealed, for the diocese often fails to fulfil its obligation to keep the building safe and weathertight, and vandalism soon reduces it to a wreck. Demolition then seems the only solution.

The shortcomings of the Pastoral Measure are painfully highlighted by the case of **St Alban's, Teddington**. This vast and once magnificent Anglo-Catholic church, built on a cathedral scale, was closed by the diocese of London in 1977, even though the Council for the Care of Churches recommended the closure of St Mary's, Teddington, instead. St Alban's was the more architecturally distinguished of the two buildings and one for which an alternative use could not easily be found. Despite this, the Church Commissioners pursued a totally impractical scheme to convert the building into squash courts and flats while, during the 'waiting period', the diocese allowed the building to be seriously vandalised. Today every window is smashed, copper has been stolen from the roof and the furnishings damaged or dispersed. An odd aspect of the case is that in 1983 a still unknown person hired a demolition company to pull the building down, although the police stopped this work before much damage was done. More recently, the diocese has been markedly uncooperative in letting people with a serious interest in using the building even have the key to inspect it. The present state of St Alban's is a disgrace which ought to be an embarrassment to the Church authorities. In January 1985 the Victorian Society published a booklet about the case, *A future for St. Alban's Teddington?*. This, for once, provoked a public reaction from the Church Commissioners, accusing the report of 'serious inaccuracies'. A further response has been a proposal finally to demolish the building.

A disturbing aspect of this case is that the advice of the Church's own expert advisory bodies has been ignored. The Victorian Society and other amenity societies therefore argue that, in the case of churches, normal statutory listed building controls should apply from the moment the building is declared redundant – even the Church's own Faculty Jurisdiction Commission advocates that 'ecclesiastical exemption' should end at the close of the three-year 'waiting period' if no alternative use has been found. Since the Church of England began to receive State aid for churches in use in 1975, some attempt has been made to conform with statutory listed building law. The possibility exists for a non-statutory public inquiry to be held to decide the fate of a redundant church for which no use can be found. Unfortunately, the operation of this concession so far suggests a lack of serious commitment by the Church to this quid pro quo for enjoying the help of public money.

In 1981 the first such non-statutory inquiry was held to decide the fate of **Holy Trinity, Rugby**, a church by Sir Gilbert Scott. It had been declared redundant in 1974 and had been extensively vandalised owing to the lack of maintenance by the diocese of Coventry. But, local and national opposition to the demolition of this potentially useful building resulted in an inquiry, at which the diocese did not deign to appear. Indeed, the diocese's behaviour was criticised in the Department of the Environment's inspector's report, which recommended delaying demolition for a year to give a local group the opportunity to acquire the building. The Secretary of State for the Environment took a tougher line and recommended that Holy Trinity should not be demolished. But, as his recommendation had no statutory force, the Church Commissioners merely waited a year and then demolished the building.

This precedent was not auspicious for the second such inquiry into a redundant church, held in May 1985. This concerned **St Wilfrid's, Brighton**, a church built in 1933–4 to the designs of the distinguished architect and historian, H. S. Goodhart-Rendel. The Thirties Society argued that it was one of the best churches of its date in the country and the Advisory Board for Redundant Churches recommended that it should go to the Fund if no alternative use could be found. Apart from the presence of asbestos acoustic plaster, which will have to be removed whether the building is demolished or not, St Wilfrid's is in good condition and suitable for alternative use. The diocese of Chichester, however, seems determined to have it down. However, the inspector recommended that St Wilfrid's should not be demolished, and the Church Commissioners have so far followed that advice.

Brighton is unfortunate as it is a town with a high proportion of Victorian churches of considerable size and significant architectural quality, so that any choice for redundancy must be regretted. Unfortunately, the church selected for closure is often the finest building in an area. Sometimes pastoral arguments clearly triumph over architectural considerations, but all too often the decision to close a particular church seems the result of Philistinism, prejudice or cynicism – as the diocese well knows, if the church is really famous, the responsibility for maintenance can be shifted on to an outside body, the Redundant Churches Fund or the taxpayer. Some of the severe criticisms of the working of the Pastoral Measure would have been mitigated had many decisions to close churches been taken after consultation with expert advisory bodies and national and local conservation societies – as should have happened with St Alban's, Teddington.

A particularly scandalous and tragic case is that of **St Edward's, Holbeck**, in Leeds. St Edward's was one of the last works of the greatest late Victorian church architect, George Frederick Bodley. It was built amid the terraces of Holbeck, an inner-city suburb of Leeds, in 1903–4 and was a building of modest scale and great refinement, which fitted into its surroundings while clearly being a church. A hall church with elegant arcades, it was of rare beauty internally and filled with furnishings of very high quality. St Edward's was first proposed for closure in 1953 but the PCC then made a strong case: 'St Edward's is a pioneer church which is literally fighting for its very existence. Its closure or amalgamation would be a blow not only to the parish but to the Catholic cause in the Church of England.' The threat of closure was only lifted in 1958, but then imposed again in 1975.

Holbeck was originally divided into three parishes. St Edward's was by far the best church both on architectural and pastoral grounds. It stood in the middle of terraced housing that had escaped the bulldozer and which is now being repaired. It was also equipped with its own church hall and parsonage house and there was a school across the road. Yet the church chosen to survive as the parish church of Holbeck was St Luke's, a mid-Victorian building of no particular quality and which, furthermore, was separated from the bulk of the population by a main road and a desert of urban clearance. St Edward's was closed in 1976. The Advisory Board for Redundant Churches considered the church was of such quality that an alternative use must be found; the Redundant Churches Fund expressed its willingness to take on the building, but the decision lay not in its hands but, as always with a redundant church, with the Church Commissioners. The parsonage house was soon sold off and after a brief career as an antique warehouse, St Edward's was allowed to stand empty and open to vandals. Those fittings not dispersed were smashed and desecrated. In its last days, the state of this beautiful building, a product of love, care and sacrifice which could still have served a useful pastoral purpose, was scarcely a good advertisement for a 'caring' Church of England, deeply concerned with the inner city. It was finally demolished by the Church Commissioners in 1984.

St Edward's may have been in part the victim of a prejudice against Anglo-Catholic churches, which were often established with small parishes in the late nineteenth century by private benefactions and which survive as a conspicuous irritation to a diocese. If true of Ripon, this is certainly true of the diocese of Manchester, which has a marked Evangelical tone. Yet this diocese, in which an alarming number of churches have been closed, furnishes one extraordinarily encouraging example of what can be achieved with a traditional church building in a blighted urban area when run by a courageous incumbent with vision and sensitivity.

**St Paul's, Salford**, is a ragstone Gothic Revival building of the 1850s of no particular architectural merit in an inner-city area which was otherwise completely redeveloped in the 1960s. It is, however, clearly a church and today is the only visible, permanent sign of the presence of God in an intimidating and depressing council estate as it stands meekly and welcomingly between tower blocks. The rector, Canon David Wyatt, chose this parish after retiring as chaplain to the Bishop of Manchester, and he was inducted in 1968 when the now run-down estate was being built. He therefore felt he had some chance of making an impression by being there at the beginning of the creation of a new community.

The old church had been kept going by a small and faithful congregation, but the building was riddled with dry rot and in an appalling structural condition. The diocese planned to replace it with a new building. 'There'll be no argument about this one,' commented the vice-chairman of the diocesan pastoral committee. Canon Wyatt did argue, however. He felt the old building was of crucial importance in the district. A petition signed by 1,900 out of the 2,000 people then living on the Ellor estate also pleaded for its retention. 'It's the only real thing around here,' one of them remarked. Canon Wyatt found an architect who agreed with him. This was Stephen Dykes Bower, architect of Bury St Edmunds cathedral, and one of the few designers alive who can deal sensitively with Victorian churches. Dykes Bower's report impressed the then bishop and the diocese eventually agreed to restore the church.

The local planning authority, however, wanted the old church down – no doubt its survival was seen as a standing reproof to the inhuman modernity of the estate which the authority had created. It took four years to get planning permission for the new wing containing the rectory and church hall which, with the church, forms two sides of a delightful walled garden which is an oasis amid the concrete. Dykes Bower designed a simple and cheap building, traditional in style: slate hung with leaded-light windows in timber frames, loosely Gothic in shape; the planners wanted something 'modern'. As for St Paul's church itself, Dykes Bower lowered the gables of the aisles to make single-pitch roofs requiring little maintenance. Inside, the interior was completely repaired and today is white and spacious, with colour introduced in stencilled patterns on the ceilings. It is furnished with fittings rescued from redundant churches with all the woodwork ebonised to introduce overall harmony. The result is a church which is numinous without being at all intimidating. The atmosphere is, as the rector says, one of joy and peace. It is also immaculately kept and is clearly loved and respected by local people. The church is left open during the day and there has only been one act of vandalism since it reopened and that was committed by an outsider. Had a new church been built it would probably look shabby, for it is the new churches built by the diocese in the 1960s which are now causing structural and maintenance problems.

The average Sunday congregation is 150 and there are, on average, forty weddings and eighty baptisms a year. This is not altogether surprising for St Paul's is not only a properly functioning parish church but is one of the few still standing in the inner districts of Salford and Manchester. The neighbouring parish, the Stowell Memorial, has now lost its church and Canon Wyatt believes that church buildings matter: 'Every time you close a church, you lose at least 80 per cent of the congregation.' In 1960 there were about 15,000 confirmations in the diocese, now there are about 3,000. He thinks it sadly ironic that, whereas in the nineteenth century Christian congregations in Britain found money to build mission churches in the Empire to try and convert pagans to Christianity, today, when Pakistanis and others move into British cities at home, the Church of England simply gives up and retreats. In Manchester, as elsewhere, the Church seems to have lost confidence and purpose, but it is wrong to think that there is no role for the Church in cities. People need religion and all that happens is that exotic and often pernicious religions spring up to fill the vacuum.

The diocese of Manchester is particularly bad in this respect. Owing to its Evangelical bias it seems to be hostile not just to Anglo-Catholic churches but to church buildings as such. The official, established, parochial role of the Church of England is abandoned and the clergy seem either obsessed with faith alone, with internal conviction which needs no building or liturgy, or with the Church as politics. In Canon Wyatt's view the only result is that ordinary people suffer. Small, self-obsessed Anglican congregations, meeting in drab surroundings or upstairs rooms are not going to make any impact in an area like Salford. 'The Church of England is in danger of losing human scale', but the presence of visible, recognisable, open church buildings gives the Church that necessary scale. St Paul's, Salford, shows that the inner city is not hopeless and that architecture matters: 'Our response to God cannot be less than physical, tangible and costly' – which is why St Paul's has been restored and beautified and why it works as a powerful symbol and a Christian presence in the middle of a planned, man-made hell. 'People believe what they see; beauty is truth.'

The Church of England would do well to contemplate this truth as it plans further retreat, further change, further dispersal of its potent legacy from the past and the closure of at least another thousand churches before the end of this century.